Manufacturing and Management

The published collection of papers given at a conference on Manufacturing and Management in December 1976 at The City University, London

**Edited by Michael Fores
and Ian Glover**

LONDON
HER MAJESTY'S STATIONERY OFFICE

© *Crown copyright 1978*
First published 1978

Design by HMSO Graphic Design

HER MAJESTY'S STATIONERY OFFICE

Government Bookshops

49 High Holborn, London WC1V 6HB
13a Castle Street, Edinburgh EH2 3AR
41 The Hayes, Cardiff CF1 1JW
Brazennose Street, Manchester M60 8AS
Southey House, Wine Street, Bristol BS1 2BQ
258 Broad Street, Birmingham B1 2HE
80 Chichester Street, Belfast BT1 4JY

Government publications are also available
through booksellers
Printed in England for Her Majesty's Stationery Office
by Page Bros (Norwich) Ltd.
Dd. 595787 K10 2/78

ISBN 0 11 512128 5

Contents

Foreword

I am pleased to have the opportunity to write the foreword to this book which discusses the important topic of 'Manufacturing and Management'.

The book represents with two exceptions the collections of papers presented to a conference on this subject arranged by the Department of Industry and held at Gresham College, The City University in December 1976.

The Conference, like those which preceded it,* arose out of the Department of Industry's general concern with the performance of the manufacturing sector. It was organised as one way of obtaining, at first hand, the views of a number of informed people from different backgrounds on the subject of the function of management in British manufacturing. Those who presented papers and the other participants covered a wide spectrum of experience in this field: manufacturing industry itself was well represented, as were consultants, business schools and universities. Moreover, the seminar had present a number of participants such as Professor Sune Carlson from Sweden, and Dr Arndt Sorge from the German Federal Republic who had made studies of various aspects of the management function in Continental Europe as well as in the United Kingdom. This, plus the presence of executives in multinational companies, served to widen the perspective of the discussions.

I think readers will find the views expressed interesting and challenging. Many of the contributions are made from original standpoints. I believe that the varied intellectual and practical disciplines of the participants serve to put British manufacturing management in a new focus.

Many of the problems which the papers identify are similar and related: not unnaturally, the solutions advocated vary; yet there are, nevertheless, certain common strands in the views expressed which have to be further explored.

Among some of the controversial propositions put forward at the Conference which readers may wish to examine, I would select the following: firstly, that the educational system in Britain in contrast to

---

* The papers of a previous conference have been published by HMSO as *Industrial efficiency and the role of government* edited by Colette Bowe.

continental countries is structured more to academic excellence than to the needs of manufacturing industry.

Secondly, that the relatively poor productivity performance of British firms could be raised, at least in part, by improved management and by executive effort.

Thirdly, that it is a mistake to view industrial management as a science. Production management is a culture of its own.

The papers were written, and are now published, to raise discussion and to try to give insight into some of the special problems of the manufacturing sector. I believe that they form a useful collection of ideas and of reports on work done, and I hope they will be read and discussed widely.

Peter Carey.

SIR PETER CAREY KCB

Permanent Secretary
Department of Industry

Introduction

Michael Fores
DEPARTMENT OF INDUSTRY

Ian Glover
THE CITY UNIVERSITY

The views expressed are personal

When the Department of Industry's conference on manufacturing and management was first planned, we asked those who were producing papers to consider the following proposition.

Together, what can be called the management movement and management science have produced a considerable body of work and put up a number of suggestions to aid in the running of units of all types. Courses have been designed to be attended by those who are employed in a range of areas: from local government, to manufacturing, to road haulage. This work has not been specific to the manufacturing sector; yet some evidence suggests that it is in manufacturing and production that some of our most pressing British economic problems lie. How can these issues be reconciled?

Manufacturing haunts the idea of management; but at the same time it is relatively neglected within business and management education. The sort of educational process sketched out in the previous paragraph often aims to deal with a typical business concern. This concern is taken to have an area within it which is called production (or manufacturing, or operations): here the product is transformed from bought-in materials and components. Yet, much of the time, management (or business) education is catering for those who do not work in a unit where anything is being manufactured.

The neglect of manufacturing in the idea of management lies, in contrast, with the fact that management education puts on fewer courses in manufacturing (or production) work, than might be predicted from the numbers of people in post. Traditionally, the typical concern has been split into two parts: with the head-office functions looking to the business schools for an educational input, and production which has looked to the engineering faculties. So we asked those producing papers for the conference to consider how useful the idea of management is in the context of the manufacturing sector.

The papers fell into four groups and were discussed in these groups. First, we had some coverage of the nature of the work of those who run manufacturing concerns and the environment of manufacturing. Second, there was an examination of the management view of events. Third, the papers considered skill and knowledge, chosen partly to see how these two aspects might best be fitted in together. The fourth session was devoted mainly to trying to synthesise elements from the earlier discussion.

In the first session, Mr Edwardes, then chairman and chief executive of Chloride Group Ltd, argued that manufacturing in Britain to-day does not have the status that manufacturing has elsewhere. But British manufacturing enterprise can be effective, if it is allowed to be;

furthermore it is effective when operating abroad. Generally our manufacturing performance has been poor for some time. High personal tax has been one constraint on improved performance, another has been too much government interference and legislation.

Critically, Mr Edwardes considers that companies in manufacturing should be concerned about making best use of their resources of people. Companies do not always take sufficient care in this way, partly because 'industry has failed to recognise that even intelligent people have different attributes'. One set of differences lies with line and staff characteristics in people and functions, factors which Chloride have researched and worked on at length.

Mr Jenkins, of ICI Petrochemicals discussed aspects of technical and engineering work in manufacturing. Jobs vary considerably, but most technical work in the chemical industry is to do with the formation of capital. Here, specialists must learn to work in teams with other specialists for long periods; so the engineer must be able to communicate easily. Management science will help most significantly when 'it encourages us to ask the right questions, and so helps us to work our way through an enormous array of variables with great inherent uncertainties'. But, most important for the subjects which contribute to management teaching, there must be a proper basis on observation of what actually happens. Thus management science must be empirically-based to be useful in practical settings.

Professor Rodger, of Heriot-Watt University, concentrated on the impact of the marketing concept on the commercial functions in the business concern. Everything that a business unit does accumulates cost, while the market is the only place where revenue is obtained. So the principal marketing contribution to management thinking has been to bring the customer closer to the 'managing nerve centre of the unit'. Marketing science has developed a number of diagnostic and analytical tools to this end, borrowing from various areas such as operational research. But the marketing function needs to be integrated with others in a systems approach to the unit; for the business concern must be considered as an integrated whole. As for teaching in the marketing area: 'The more post-experience students, the better. . . But our present higher education system is geared to school-leavers.'

For the second session of the December 1976 conference, on 'the management tradition', Professor Child, of Aston University, who is the author of one of the best books on the subject, *British Management Thought,* chose to speak about a research investigation; he reported on what seems to be a case of white-collar overmanning in the manufacturing sector. Mr Mant and Dr Sorge, however, both looked directly at the management idea. The former presented a chapter of his book which is now published, *The Rise and Fall of the British Manager;* so we have substituted, for this, the result of a piece of research done by Mr Mant for the Department and completed in 1977. Dr Sorge has looked at the management idea from a German perspective, his experience being based on his participation in an Anglo–Franco–German comparitive study of the structure of manufacturing concerns.

Professor Child introduced his paper in the context of the Bacon and Eltis 'too few producers' debate for Britain. Bacon and Eltis have been concerned that there has been a 'long-term shift of expenditure and employment to the non-productive sector'; but they neglect the 'non-producers' within the manufacturing sector. Professor Child has extended C Northcote Parkinson's famous analysis of administrative proliferation in the public sector to a part of the private sector. He has found the same tendency in a large British manufacturing group, and suggests 'the indirect component within the productive sector is growing more than proportionately' with growing specialization. His findings can be read with the observation of Mr Glover's first paper that only Britain, of the European countries, has a strong perception of separate groups called professions; only Britain has the proliferation of specialist groups that this perception seems to accompany.

Mr Mant, an independent consultant, argued at the conference that British culture, in the post-war period, has shown strong evidence of being dependent on American ideas. Tenets, such as those of management ideology, had to be of American origin to seem legitimate. In his paper in this book, Mr Mant reports the results of a study of the experience of multi-national companies which operate manufacturing subsidiaries in Britain and elsewhere. British productivity is usually rather low by the standards of other developed countries. One reason for this is that British managers seem to be more interested in general factors, such as status, and 'industrial relations', than in the specific features of jobs. So, Britons tend to relate to each other without sufficient concern with the shared task. 'Seen thus, the current emphasis on human relations in industry may be misconceived, unless it is set in the context of task, role and authority.' A way out of our problems may be to revert to 'old wisdom', and rediscover a type of leadership in manufacturing concerns which is 'rough but fair', and especially concerned with the task and the product. Mr Mant sees the need for there to be fights within manufacturing concerns; but they need to be in the right places.

Dr Sorge, now with the International Institute of Management in Berlin, has been engaged on the British end of the study already mentioned. In his paper, he argued that the 'management' idea is less attractive in Germany than Britain. Traditionally those who want to go into the manufacturing sector have specialised in full-time higher, and other post-school, education on subjects which relate to their future work. They have become either a *Techniker* (engineer) or a *Kaufmann* (commercial man), and centres of management education have had little part in this process. German manufacturing concerns rely heavily on engineers to staff higher executive jobs across a range of functions. Criticisms that Germany has a 'management gap', because of the weakness of formal management training, can be countered by arguing that other arrangements are available to produce those who can run business concerns effectively. In particular, 'the idea of management as a profession does not occur' in Germany.

In third session of the conference, on skill and knowledge, Professor Hudson, now of Brunel University, took a case-study of entrepreneurship in manufacturing, and followed up an earlier paper which he produced for the Department on the entrepreneur as a 'prime mover' whose particular skills lie in making room for himself to be able to operate. Mr Glover, of the City University, examined the utility of the professional model of behaviour for executive work in manufacturing concerns. Professor Carlson, of Uppsala University, who was the first person to have examined what executives really do, used his experience of being a member of a number of boards to discuss the effect of language on the selection and use of information in business concerns.

Professor Hudson's case-study comes from the eighteenth century, and his own long-lasting interest in the expression of human talent. Young Britons tend to think of factories as being 'dirty' places, unfit to be workplaces for 'gentlemen'. But a man like Nicholas Sprimont, originally a silversmith, could make a product which was fine in quality and successful commercially. 'Chelsea porcelain of the red anchor period can stand comparison with any porcelain made.' Sprimont, who ran the factory, seems to have been inspired by the risky nature of the challenge facing him. He was also an outsider, to the type of business and to the country. Manufacturing 'remains an activity of special excitement'; and there is a regeneration to-day of interest in the craft tradition. Manufacturing concerns ought to be able to use these factors to attract able people.

Mr Glover, of The City University, has put forward a thesis stemming from the proposition that those who have called for British manufacturing to become more 'professional' have not always offered prescriptions which make it more efficient. The idea of professionalism is, even more so than that of 'management', uniquely a strong one in Britain amongst the European countries. The professional model of behaviour has been based on one which has a long history but was adopted first by those who gave advice in the service sector, rather than by people who ran manufacturing concerns. 'The archetypal professional is the lawyer or the doctor. His origins are those of a smalltown big-shot from eighteenth-century, pre-industrial life.' The mismatch between professionalism and manufacturing enterprise stems partly from the fact that professional people stress direct responsibility, in their work, to the local community; whereas manufacturers produce for the world. Professionalism stresses static qualities associated with advisers sitting at desks; business executives live more fragmented and hectic lives. Besides this, our British liking for professionalism has led to a 'proliferation of occupations (which) is quite remarkable'; we have invented groups like quantity surveyors for which Continental European countries see no need at all. One way around this problem is to adopt some Continental habits, especially giving the qualification function to full-time education so that the education sector will learn to concentrate more on skills used in workplaces outside education.

It was Professor Carlson, of the University of Uppsala, Sweden, whose book, *Executive Behaviour,* first showed, in 1951, that the pattern of executive work is typically quite different from that which executives themselves think it to be. An executive, when asked about his work, will tend to describe an ideal day, which bears little resemblance to the details of a typical day. In his paper for this book, Professor Carlson argues another case which is sceptical of a piece of unresearched, received wisdom about a feature of executive work.

In reality, 'most top executives do not form their opinions on information, as it was assumed earlier, but on other people's opinions'. Before the publication of *Executive Behaviour,* commentators liked to picture the top executive of a company as a planner; whereas in fact his role is often more that of a firefighter. The executive is not desk-bound, like Mr Glover's typical professionals tend to be, but someone who moves from pillar to post. In his paper Professor Carlson points out that the top executive picks up his information in ways which are not so ordered. He is dependent both on the language and the symbols adopted for information flows, also on translation of these flows from language to language. Knowledge of all sorts is important for the company, but accounting practice rates it as 'a rather dubious asset'; and top executives 'rarely get any information directly by observation of facts or events on the spot'.

One of the last two papers was discussed at the final session of the conference in December 1976. The other, Mr Glover's second paper, accents international comparisons. It is based on a summary of work done for the Department of Industry to try to establish the backgrounds, qualifications and career patterns of those running manufacturing concerns in Britain, France, Germany and Sweden.

Mr Fores, of the Department of Industry, argued from the proposition that, although science is useful to those running concerns in manufacturing, the scientist is not normally the best person to run them. Scientific work and executive work in business have quite different modes, as Professor Hudson's, Professor Carlson's and Mr Glover's first paper all show. Factors which are the vital ones for running businesses are intangibles, associated with art and skill: intuition, imagination, inspiration, personal 'flair'. Hard, scientific knowledge is needed by executives, if it is available; but the world which they face is to a considerable degree unknown and unknowable. Some of management science and management writing has not taken full account of this feature. Neither has it taken full account of the fact that detail, especially artifact-detail and market-detail, is normally more important than principle in manufacturing.

The model of a House of Science is put forward to show how knowledge transfers from the scientist to the manufacturer, and how formal knowledge can be useful in all parts of the concern. When the manufacturer looks for scientific knowledge to improve his operation, he has to shop around to find it in any part of science.

Mr Glover's second paper argues that career patterns for executives in manufacturing concerns are different in Britain, compared with the other three countries examined: France, Germany and Sweden. There are more executives who have gone through formal higher education in the other three countries. Continental and Swedish executives are more likely to have studied a subject which seems relevant to work in manufacturing than their British counterparts. Production is relatively less popular in Britain. 'Britain's system of matching education and jobs was not moulded in the philosophy that the needs of industry were very important.' In consequence, we lack 'a modern system for ensuring that a good proportion of (our) most able people reach top positions in manufacturing industry'. To alleviate these weaknesses, Mr Glover makes some suggestions, which include less specialization in secondary schools and the use of teaching staff with experience of work outside the educational environment.

There are some common themes running through a number of the papers in this book. One is Mr Jenkins' argument that, because executive work and work undertaken by managers varies so much between jobs, management and business education should be geared to specific requirements as much as possible. Despite these differences, however, Professor Rodger is surely right to depict the company as a unit in which costs are incurred everywhere; it is only in the market where revenue is obtained. Mr Edwardes' comments about inherent differences between line and staff jobs can be considered with Mr Glover's comments on the professions; the typical professional mode of work may be more suitable for staff jobs than those in the line. Mr Mant's thesis that British executives are less concerned with the task in hand than Continental European counterparts may be influenced by our particular ideas of professionalism.

Professor Hudson, Professor Carlson and Mr Fores all try to picture executive work as being concerned with risk in a regime where too little is known. Professor Child's evidence on white-collar over-manning can be read with the Anglo-German comparison that we have occupational groups for which the Germans see no need. Dr Sorge's argument that the 'management' idea has not caught on much in Germany is worth special consideration; the business schools in Britain and America are perhaps doing a sort of conversion job, to compensate for the fact that English-speaking recruits to manufacturing concerns have followed courses which are less directly useful for executive work than is the case in most of Continental Europe, where the German-inspired system tends to operate.

British industry and industry in Britain

Michael Edwardes
BRITISH LEYLAND

The author is chairman of British Leyland. When this paper was written, he was chairman and chief executive of Chloride Group Ltd

Introduction

One must accept that in the United Kingdom at present, manufacturing industry does not have the status and stature that it does in other western countries. Reasons advanced, both real and imaginary, include:

(a) The economic and social environment within which industry in this country operates.

(b) Industry's evident lack of success at home is often attributed to ineffective management.

(c) The personal taxation system, which discourages work and study put in to earn promotion, productivity bonuses, overtime, etc.

(d) The risk/reward package which no longer works in favour of private industry – as opposed to the public sector.

(e) The apparent lack of intellectual stimulus and creativity associated with industry.

(f) The orientation of education towards the arts and the professions rather than to engineering and manufacture.

(g) The working conditions and locations associated with factories.

The underlying premise in this paper is that British management can be very effective when it is allowed to be effective. However, industry can improve upon its utilisation of people resources. Unless we in industry improve our ability to use managers – 'break' fewer managers – we may well continue to lose good people – people of high intelligence, with drive and potential – to what some of us may feel to be more comfortable vocations!

We need to distinguish between British Industry and industry in Britain. There is a difference between managing companies in a country such as the United Kingdom, where the socio/economic climate inhibits investment and profitability – and in overseas countries which set out to create a climate conducive to investment and profitability. Our record of British industry based in other countries is excellent – our record of industry (whether British or otherwise) based in Britain, is patchy.

British Industry as compared with industry in Britain

Before analysing the constraints upon and deficiencies of British industrial management – it is well worth comparing the economic record of United Kingdom industry at home and abroad.

Figure 1.1   UK industrial and commercial companies pre-tax rates of return 1960–75

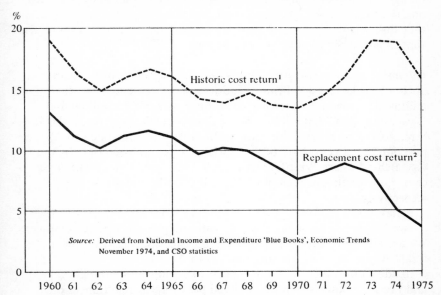

1   Gross trading profits plus rent received less capital consumption at historic cost as percentage of net fixed capital
    stock in the UK at historic cost plus book value of stocks.

2   Gross trading profits plus rent received less stock appreciation and capital consumption at replacement cost as
    percentage of net fixed capital stock in the UK at replacement cost plus book value of stocks.

The United Kingdom's industrial track record   Profitability in United
Kingdom industry has declined steadily from a return (on replacement
cost) of an inadequate 13 per cent in 1960 to an abysmal 4 per cent in
1975 (*see* Figure 1.1).

Britain's share of world manufacturing exports has declined from
18 per cent to 9 per cent in the 17 years ending 1975, and having gained
in penetration in 1976 with our staggering devaluation, is probably at
no more than 10 per cent.

Britain's annual growth in manufacturing investment in the period
1960–73 at 2.1 per cent compares unfavourably with the German 4.3
per cent, the French 7.8 per cent, and the Japanese 11.1 per cent. This
is despite the fact that equity funds have been generously available over
the years (with the exception of short periods of famine) and so 'the
City' has not been the limiting factor.

In 1975, 59 000 people in administration, managerial and technical
categories emigrated from the United Kingdom. The figure has
increased from 32 500 in 1972 and 39 000 in 1974. Executives, middle

managers and skilled workers all realise that the economic freeze and a falling standard of living can be put behind them; especially in Africa and the Middle East. Multi-national companies find that not only are they losing key people from their United Kingdom operations, but also that expatriates will not be attracted back.

Britain's world-wide record   This is another matter. British ownership of capital stock outside Britain – now valued at around $24000 million – is second only to the USA. France with $9500 million and Germany with $7300 million are third and fourth respectively. This is reinforced by recent figures for world investment income which show that our 12 per cent share of the world total is surpassed only by the USA. Behind us are West Germany with 7 per cent, France with 6 per cent, Japan with 5 per cent and the Netherlands with 4 per cent respectively.

Britain is the largest foreign investor in the United States where we compete aggressively and effectively with indigenous American industry. We are also the most effective foreign investors in countries such as India, Australia, New Zealand and South Africa.

In addition to British visible exports of around £19000 million pa and invisible exports of around £8700 pa, overseas remittances on investments aggregate some £1600 million pa.

British managers and other skilled categories are welcomed with open arms in North America, the 'old' Commonwealth and Europe. The fact that so many British managers attain high positions in industry in other parts of the world is further evidence of their inherent competence.

The fact that our record outside the United Kingdom is very much better than our performance at home suggests that the economic environment in Britain is not hospitable to industry. Successive governments have failed to create an industrial climate which tempts investment at home: investment grants, tax concessions, etc, simply do not off-set inadequate profitability and lack of people-incentives. The relationship between profitability and investment is demonstrated at Figure 1.2 for the United Kingdom and at Figure 1.3 for Chloride.

Constraints affecting industry in Britain

In the United Kingdom the effects of progressively rising personal tax rates dissuade hourly paid operatives from earning overtime and productivity bonuses and inhibit managers from working for (or even

Figure 1.2 UK industrial and commercial companies – changes in profits and investment (current prices)

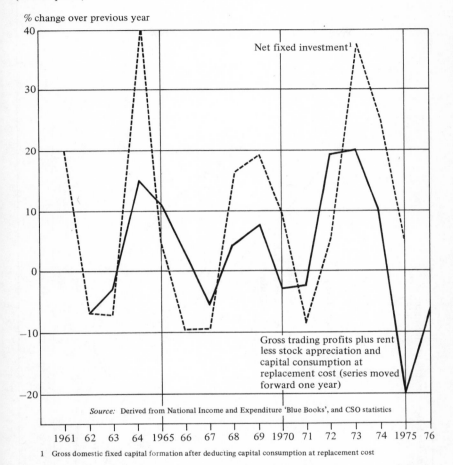

% change over previous year

Net fixed investment[1]

Gross trading profits plus rent less stock appreciation and capital consumption at replacement cost (series moved forward one year)

Source: Derived from National Income and Expenditure 'Blue Books', and CSO statistics

1961 62 63 64 1965 66 67 68 69 1970 71 72 73 74 1975 76

1   Gross domestic fixed capital formation after deducting capital consumption at replacement cost

accepting) promotion. The net after-tax income is often felt not to compensate for the time spent away from family or leisure pursuits, or for the additional responsibility. To underline the point, the top rate of personal tax on earned income in the United Kingdom is 83 per cent (98 per cent on unearned income)–which compares to France 49 per cent, USA 50 per cent and Germany 56 per cent. See Table 1.1 for a personal tax comparison with other industrial countries and see Table 1.2 for the percentage of tax deducted from incomes in the United Kingdom.

Figure 1.3 Chloride – the relationship between profit and investment

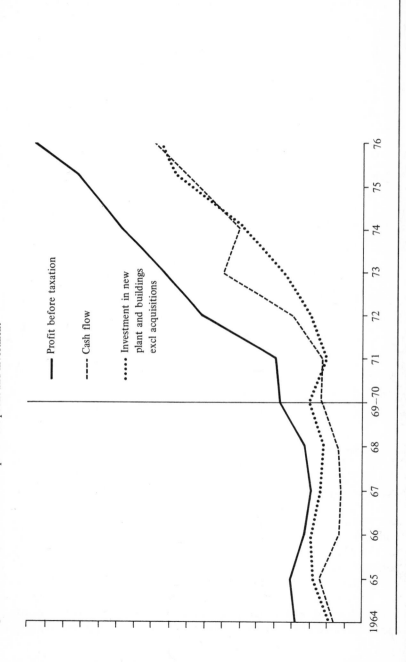

Table 1.1   Income taxes and social security contributions comparative examples

The following tables compares the net annual take-home pay (after Income Taxes and Social Security contributions) as a percentage of earnings:

Earnings £	United Kingdom %	France %	Germany %	USA %
Married man with two children				
4000	73	94	77	90
6000	70	90	75	84
10000	62	85	72	80
15000	53	80	66	76
20000	46	76	62	73
25000	41	74	59	70
Married man with no children				
4000	68	86	69	86
6000	66	84	67	81
10000	59	78	65	77
15000	51	74	61	74
20000	44	71	58	71
25000	39	69	56	68

Source: Eurocom Management Centre report, *1976 Statutory and Occupational Benefit Programmes in Europe and Related Tax Aspects.*
US $ converted at $2 = £1.

Table 1.2   Effective rates of income tax plus social security contributions for a married man with two children under 11. With income (all earned) expressed as a multiple of average male earnings.

Multiple of average	1964/65 %	1970/71 %	1973/74 %	1976/77 %
1	9.5	20.0	18.8	24.8
2	19.3	24.6	25.0	31.4
3	22.9	27.7	26.7	38.1
4	24.7	31.2	30.1	44.8
5	26.5	35.5	34.2	50.2
10	37.9	53.7	49.3	65.8

Source: The Budgetary Situation: An Appraisal
Professor Robert Neild, 1976
Department of Applied Economics, University of Cambridge
Notes: Average male earnings, 1976 c £3350 pa

The growth of the public sector work-forces, with their inflation proofed pensions and security of employment, combined with comparable remuneration, has attracted potentially dynamic people away from the hurly-burly of manufacturing industry, which once offered greater rewards to make up for the lack of security. Remuneration standards, terms of employment, and working attitudes are to an extent set by public employment.

The following details of salary offered to graduates in large industrial firms, and civil service salary scales have been extracted from *The Times* (6.8.76).

(a) Likely graduate earnings in larger industrial firms:

Age	Salary band £
25	3 550 – 4 200
30	5 650 – 6 750
35	7 300 – 8 500
40	8 250 – 9 800

(b) Civil Service salary scales – administrative grade:

Grade	Likely age on promotion	Salary band £
Admin trainee	21	2 707 – 3 982
Principal	28 – 29	5 992 – 7 762
Assistant Secretary	36 – 42	8 650 – 11 000

The exceptionally high wage awards (before the freeze period) – not only exacerbated inflation, making us far less competitive industrially, but they also eroded differentials to the clear disadvantage of skilled people in management or technical roles. Quite apart from the fact that the wage awards were harmful to the national interest in themselves, they triggered off other unhelpful side effects. Labour productivity fell – and for subsequent wage controls to be credible, government in its wisdom saw the need to limit dividends. Dividends today, after inflation, are 27 per cent lower per share than they were ten years ago! Using the same measure, wage earnings per head are 34 per cent higher.

The effect of this social restructuring has been counter-productive. Investment in manufacturing industry on the part of pensioners and savers, whether individuals or institutions, has been inhibited because they rely on a dividend yield which is now very much less than can be offered by those non-wealth creating sectors of the economy which compete for their funds. Even when funds are available, the erosion of differentials disenchants those scarce people who drive investments through – because their standards of living were not protected by union muscle during the 'grab all' period. For example front line managers were left behind and as a direct consequence there has been a surge of unionisation of front line managers in the past 3 to 4 years.

There is no doubt that industry must carry a great deal of the blame for giving in to excessive claims from some sectors of employees while at the same time allowing the remuneration position of its managers and other skilled people from shopfloor to boardroom, to be eroded. There is no doubt that this has been a factor in the low intake of engineers.

The emigration of so many skilled people can be partly attributed to the fact that people now focus on after-tax income – high tax rates are an even more significant factor than low gross salary levels in Britain.

As government believes that it knows best, it tries more and more to regulate industry, and it demands more and more information. The manager sees less and less occurring as a direct consequence of his own actions.

The high level of public expenditure has been funded by a mixture of high personal tax and increased public sector borrowing. The first demotivates those who determine investment; the second forces the government to offer high interest rates to protect the pound which is always under pressure from critical holders of sterling. High interest rates make capital investment projects less viable.

With interest costs often double those prevailing in overseas countries (such as Germany or the USA) the cost of money is simply not competitive. Interest rates of up to 18 per cent compare with returns (on replacement cost) of under 4 per cent. It is easier and more lucrative to invest in government securities – rather than manufacturing plant.

As a corporate incentive to invest in 'making things' has been inhibited by price control, restrictive union practices, and the combination of government interference and excessive legislation – so the incentive for people to choose a career in management is likewise diluted.

Some remedies to the constraints

Reduce rates of personal tax down to those prevailing in competitor countries (*see* Table 1.1). The reduced tax yield can be compensated for by an increase in indirect taxation, or better still by reduction in public expenditure to levels that our economy can support.

A suggested schedule of Marginal Rates (which is shown in comparison with the 1975/76 Marginal Rates) could be as follows:*

Taxable income per annum	1975/76 marginal income tax rate	Suggested marginal income tax rate
Up to £5000	35%	35.0%
£5000 to £5500	40%	
£5500 to £6500	45%	37.5%
£6500 to £7500	50%	
£7500 to £8500	55%	40.0%
£8500 to £10000	60%	
£10000 to £12000	65%	42.5%
£12000 to £15000	70%	
£15000 to £20000	75%	45.0%
£20000 and above to £25000	83%	47.5%
£25000 and above		50.0%

* Courtesy of Sir Emmanuel Kaye, October 1976

The cost of the above reductions would amount to some £760 million pa. Those of us who read our papers on Monday, 15 November, 1976 will remember, perhaps with horror, that the triggering off of adjustments to social benefits that day, were estimated to cost the country an extra £1400 million pa.

Public sector remuneration and terms of employment simply must not be allowed to run ahead of the private sector.

Companies can and should increase individuals' salaries, (in preference to providing bonuses and enhancing fringe benefits!) where performance merits it. What they should not do, is simply pay the average going rate when individual performance is above par, or below par. Thus incentives have to be demonstrable and attainable. And with promotion goes additional responsibility. The additional responsibility has to be compensated for by realistic, after-tax, pay differentials.

Call a halt to the flow of legislation. Smaller businesses simply can't cope with the burden of the range and depth of legislation – and big companies cope only by increasing their non-productive costs.

The Price Commission should certainly be dispensed with, for in a recession it has been demonstrated as unnecessary due to the competitive position engendered by industry's spare capacity – and in a boom it holds down profitability and hence funds for subsequent investment.

Reduce public expenditure to within 40 per cent to 50 per cent of GNP and thereby reduce both public sector borrowing – and taxation.

Only when the government creates a business climate conducive to profitability (. . . and hence investment) and reinstates personal rewards, will the effectiveness of management increase: particularly if personal rewards for merit, from the shopfloor to the boardroom, are allowed to be allied to the productivity or profitability of the operation.

People resources

Whatever the political and economic environment, what people resources we have need to be optimised, and the challenge of motivating people in an unhelpful environment is, of course, greater than ever.

Recruitment and deployment of key resources becomes critical to the very survival of industry in Britain.

Recruitment and deployment   Matching the job to be filled and the job-holder's future prospects with the attributes and skills of the applicants, necessitates a full understanding of the respective skills and attributes of the applicants. This is best achieved by a corporate management resources function – which is concerned with all the aspects of recruitment, deployment, monitoring, advising on pro-motions, transfers, compensation of senior managers and highly skilled people. Not all companies in Britain have a specific management resources function, and the absence of this approach often makes it difficult to harness management talent effectively.

Our own management resources function has direct responsibility for the 70 top managers – we employ a total of 22 000 people around the world – and an indirect co-ordinating role for a further 400. We have been able to identify and attract non-British talent to certain top jobs in Britain, where cross-fertilisation of thinking has been particularly important. We operate what we call a people-oriented appointment policy, rather than a succession-oriented policy, which is based on the premise that the development of an individual with talent will rebound to the benefit of the company, so that his career path may sometimes take priority over immediate optimisation from the pure succession point of view.

If choosing the second best internal applicant, in order to give him vital career experience, strengthens the total team at the next stage, that later synergy is worth short term sacrifice. But this whole subject flows into the question of involving people, and in particular involving managers.

Involvement   A great deal is being said today about industrial democracy – in Chloride we prefer to describe our approach as one of employee-involvement. The concept of worker control is a nonsense. When one is developing managers because of their potential and their skill – to supersede the manager's decision making role by structured worker control is self-defeating. On the other hand, we believe that employees have a right to be consulted on strategic decisions that affect their livelihood. We would not put forward a major industrial investment to our Main Board without comprehensive discussion with the employees concerned. This can be tedious, and it can take many months; this can be frustrating. Nevertheless we believe that it is in the company's enlightened self-interest for all concerned to be committed to a strategic course of action.

Having said this, one of the attitude problems which industry in Britain faces, is lack of manager-involvement. When one thinks of the media coverage that has been given to worker involvement, one cannot help a wry smile when one thinks of the number of companies who do not seriously involve their managers in the decision making process!

Our own approach to this is to start by committing our directors, executives, managers and all employees to an overall philosophy which is set out in our Board Policy Statement – see Appendix 1. This policy document embraces, for example, corporate responsibility to stake-holders, areas of business activity, organisation and financing. At the same time we encourage our executives to develop their own management style within our involvement philosophy, for the obvious reason that encouraging individuals' entrepreneurial spirit within a framework of proper disciplines, helps to motivate them.

Involvement at Chloride is maintained by formal meetings of Group entities (panels or policy committees) and by frequent informal contact between managers. By utilising committees to review investment proposals, management resources, technology and strategy we enable a wide range (and depth) of people to be involved in the shaping of policy and in decision making.

By maintaining a small central communications function at our headquarters and by appointing a manager at each company responsible for communications, we have been able not only to present ourselves to the outside world but also to keep employees informed of what is happening specifically at their company and more generally throughout the Group – and to achieve the vital feed-back of thinking without which passing of information does not graduate to 'communication.'

People are different

A great deal of the time of top industrial people today is spent in trying
to get across to politicians, civil servants and the education system, what
it is that they can do to improve the situation so that industry in
Britain can be as effective as British industry is outside Britain, and as
our international competitors are in their various countries. However,
industry has a great deal to answer for, and in particular one feels that
the more intelligent individual, including the graduate, is not always
used effectively. I doubt whether figures are available, but one suspects
that many intelligent people have been lost to industry because they
were misplaced or under-used while in industry. There is an apparent
lack of intellectual stimulus and creativity associated with industry –
partly because industry has failed to recognise that even intelligent
people have different attributes.

In my view this is because companies are not explicit about the
distinction between staff and line. Companies are often not deliberately
selective in ensuring that line people are used in line jobs and staff
people in staff jobs. Line and staff functions and individuals in Chloride
are described as follows.

Line and staff functions   A line function is primarily concerned with
directing or managing others to achieve objectives which relate directly
to the creation of wealth. A line function invariably involves decision
making.

A staff function is primarily concerned with advising, recommending,
or providing specialist and or general support to those whose roles are
specifically concerned with wealth creation. A staff function may or
may not involve decision making.

Staff and line – the individual   A staff-oriented individual is one whose
attributes and characteristics are more compatible with the role of
advising, recommending or providing specialist or general support to
others, than with the role of leading, directing or managing. He may or
may not be a competent decision-maker, but his judgement needs to be
good.

A line-oriented individual is one whose attributes and characteristics
are more compatible with the role of leading, directing or managing
others, than with the role of advising, recommending or providing
specialist or general support. A line-oriented executive must be a
competent decision maker, relying as appropriate on the judgement of
competent staff men.

The fact that individuals are staff-oriented or line-oriented, to whatever degree, does not indicate the level at which an individual is capable of operating. Line or staff characteristics are not 'better' or 'worse' – merely different.

How Chloride harness the staff and line attributes of their employees
A deliberate attempt is made to achieve a balance of staff and line input throughout Chloride's decision making processes. These balanced entities enhance the objectivity of decision making, and achieve greater commitment, so that decisions will be made and implemented effectively. They also help to filter the nature and number of decisions which are required to be made by executive directors, the chief executive and Main Board.

Chloride have found that it is important to analyse the nature of the entity and of the functions, and certainly of the individual, if management resources are to be harnessed within the Group organisation. For example, the Main Board as an entity has a line role, yet it needs to be made up of both line and staff people if it is to be effective. A job function on the other hand which is line in nature invariably requires a line-oriented individual, whereas a staff function requires someone with staff-oriented characteristics. Indeed a heavily line-oriented person operating in an expert staff role may well be unhappy in this role and will probably be a source of irritation to his colleagues, and so in the long run ineffective.

On all the Group Boards and committees provision is made for both line and staff input:
(a) At the Main Board the line input comes from the chief executive and the three regional managing directors whereas the staff input comes from the chairman and the other directors.
(b) All the advisory bodies to the chief executive, embracing:
Top Management, Investment appraisals, Management Resources and Technology, are balanced in terms of line and staff.
(c) In addition to the balance between line and staff executive directors on the subsidiary Boards, Chloride have some 110 non-executive directors in the Group, who make an important local contribution to these Boards world-wide.
(d) The balance between line and staff is well established at company level, where one of the criteria for management appointment is the analysis, by in-depth psychological assessment, of the degree to which the particular individual is 'line' or 'staff'. General Managers will invariably need to be more line-oriented than staff, whereas personnel directors will normally tend to be staff-oriented. However, there are

deliberate exceptions; for example, where a line manager is placed in a staff role or a staff manager in a line role for the purpose of career development, or to give a particular bias to a job that needs to be done for a specific purpose, and for a limited period of time.

As stated earlier, we in industry must improve our ability to use managers – 'break' fewer managers – to ensure that we do not continue to lose good people.

Conclusion

There is much that can and must be done by management in industry to manage better, and by union members and other employees to reduce restrictive practices, however fairly bargained for in the first place! But there is no way that industry in Britain will make the grade unless Government:

(a) Reduces public expenditure to reduce the high level of interest rates – and see (d).

(b) Allows dividends to compete with the yields that investors can obtain from Government and other competitors for funds.

(c) Permits prices to fluctuate according to the market economy, to ensure that companies have the profits and therefore the funds to invest, and the will to invest.

(d) Allows incentives to be applied – from the shopfloor to the Board-room – by sharply reducing the rates of personal direct taxation.

(e) Encourages proper pay differentials to enable merit and 'time investment' to be rewarded – adequately.

(f) Refrains from excessive de-motivating intervention in private and public enterprise.

All else is largely peripheral. We must put right these obvious areas which contribute to Britain being so inhospitable to industry!

The nature of management work: the technical function

B T Jenkins
ICI PETROCHEMICALS DIVISION

The author is Personnel and Site Co-ordinating
Director Wilton

B

Before embarking on a description of 'the technical function' and the relationship between the job activity and management science, it would be helpful to make two general points which establish the context of the argument.

The first point (which is often overlooked) is that 'industry' is very diverse. There are many different patterns of activity, differing technologies and different business environments, all of which affect the organisation and style of a business enterprise; so generalisations must be treated with scepticism. The chemical industry itself is far from homogeneous, and what follows is based on experience in petrochemicals. This sector is characterised by very capital intensive large-scale operations: each new plant represents investment in terms of millions of pounds sterling. The costs of operation are heavily dependent on raw materials and energy and the break-even point is often about three-quarters the rated capacity of the plant. The market is international, so that the logistics of distribution are important. Commercial operations are made even more complex because the manufacturing units are highly interdependent. The output of plant A is often a saleable product in its own right, but serves also as the starting point for a second unit taking that product and converting it to another product, which in turn can be sold or used as the feedstock for yet a third plant, and so on. There is thus a long chain from, say, crude oil through to fibres or plastics end products.

The second point is semantic: 'management science' is a very woolly phrase and, for the purpose of this paper, the loose definition will be used of 'a corpus of knowledge which can be applied to the organisation and performance of an enterprise'. The looseness is quite deliberate, in that the definition includes those areas of knowledge which enable managers to gain insights, and ask the right questions. We are not therefore limited solely to those branches of management science which claim to enable managers to arrive at quantitative predictions based on 'hard' input data. In other words, we are including within our definition the whole broad area of organisation theory and the various conceptual models which have been developed for the analysis of organisational behaviour – for example, the very interesting work of Beer which has been helpful in at least one application of which the author has personal experience.

The nature of technical work

Having made those two general observations, we can now turn to the nature of technical work in this branch of industry. Surprisingly, perhaps, the major task of the technical function is to assist in the formation of capital. This is a critical part of the business and here some recent figures may be quoted to support the point. The addition of the necessary extra capacity may represent, in one are of business, the investment of £140 million, in another £90 million, in yet another £150 million. Wrong judgement of the market, uncritical appreciation of the technology can lead to crippling or, at least, debilitating losses. Even where the 'technical function' is applied to existing production operations, it is mainly focused on plant modifications directed towards increased output or greater efficiency, and thus represents the addition of further capital. For reasons of safety and efficiency, most production operations are highly automated and most of the technically capable manager's time there is claimed by problems of man-management or administration.

How then do we go about organising technical talent in the service of capital formation? It should be remembered that different disciplines are involved in the process of moving from a chemical idea to the construction of an operational plant. New products and processes are the brain children of chemists, often stimulated by data about gaps in markets supplied by marketing and commercial specialists. The first step in turning these ideas into operational plant is taken by the chemical engineers, who design the industrial scale unit processes. These in turn have to be developed into hardware – pumps, vessels, control systems, which are designed by mechanical, electrical and instrument engineers.

To preserve the liveliness and expertise of these specialists, it has been, and will long remain, the practice to organise them into separate operational units – Research and Development Departments, Technical and Engineering Departments and so on, with the commercial expertise supplied by Marketing Department. This functional organisation is spanned by the 'integrated' project teams, which, in ways not easily expressed by organisation charts, combine the disciplines required in varying proportions at the various stages of the project. At the latter stages of the project, there will be a heavy involvement of the construction engineer and the Works people who will be responsible for commissioning and operating the plant.

The total process from chemical idea to completed plant takes at least five years, and sometimes longer if the technology is unproven.

Commercially, it is vital that the market is right for the product when the plant comes on stream, and there is obviously enormous uncertainty in trying to gauge the market five to ten years ahead. There is, therefore, a considerable inducement to devise predictive models, some of which are of considerable complexity, to determine market movements against the background of various trade cycles and movements in international trade, but there is no doubt that a vital factor still is the judgement of very experienced managers. It is fashionable now to decry corporate planning but, as military strategists have long realised, the essence of long-range planning is that it is kept under continual review. It has been wisely observed that the benefits of planning stem from the process of doing it – the examination of assumptions, the definition and consideration of options. It is this dialogue which is the important thing, rather than an end result comprising a neatly bound 'corporate plan', outdated before it has been printed.

The role of management science

Uncertainty is inevitable and one management scientist has defined it as the difference between the amount of information available at the beginning of a task and the amount required to complete it. Here, one has to deal with a huge amount of information between the initial concept and the actual plant producing many thousands of tonnes of product per year. This requires that the chemist, chemical engineer, mechanical and instrument engineer, safety engineer, construction engineer, operations people and marketing people have knowledge and appreciation of each other's problems. They must not only tolerate each other's viewpoint, but converse constructively so as to enable the project to grow and to achieve excellence from their association.

It is precisely at this point, where technologies impinge one on another, that the management sciences have grown up. Systems engineering, 'project management', PERT, critical path scheduling and so on, have been developed whereby many resources are combined under time pressure. The impulse behind them all has been the need to integrate the specialisms in the execution of a common task.

Thus a 'manager' in this system of capital formation must certainly pursue with vigour the disciplines of his speciality. But that, in itself, is not enough. He must be capable of listening to, and responding to, his colleague of other displines, another interest. More, their interaction should produce a better result than they could independently contrive – 'synergy'. Let us take a few examples.

Case 1   Market Development Manager   The 'Accountabilities' in the written job description comprise items of this kind:
'Identify opportunities for new products, develop new products required and define potential markets.'
'Ensure the cost effectiveness of new products, defining their technical advantages in terms of selling price and applications.' These are phrased very much in individual terms, but the other items emphasise collaborative aspects of the job:
'Secure Divisional commitment and resources to an action plan. . . .'
'Develop the project to (application for capital sanction) working in close collaboration with other functions within the Division. . . .'
'Plan in detail market strategy in collaboration with Marketing Department. . . .'

Case 2   Manager, product X new processes   The purpose of the job is to discover and develop new and more economic routes to product X. However, we find that not only must he keep abreast of new developments elsewhere (this follows very directly from the stated purpose) but also
'The job holder's main activities are to create the environment within which innovation can flourish. . . .'
'To ensure the relevance of the Department's work to the Division aims. . . .'
'To design and modify project teams, balancing individual needs and abilities.'
'Represent the section at planning and review meetings and keep the section in touch with and responsible to changes in policy or opinion.'
'He has to initiate working arrangements with other relevant groups, take part in setting up ad hoc joint working arrangements when necessary.'

Case 3   Project Technical Manager   Purpose – 'Define the Division's needs for new plant to manufacture product Y and related products in terms of size, location, timing and technology, and prepare expenditure proposals for Board approval'. Here, surely par excellence, the technical job – But what follows?
'Integration with the activities of other Departments is an essential feature of the job. Whereas in the initial stages of a contract, the emphasis is on commercial and economic aspects requiring liaison and co-ordination with Marketing, Supply and Accountancy Department, it subsequently moves to consideration of technical aspects with Research and Development, Production and Engineering Departments. There is a continuous close relationship with Secretary's Department on legal/contractual matters and statutory requirements. . . . The Job

Holder's accountabilities are mainly discharged by working with groups of people from other Departments, frequently as team leader, even though other members of the team may enjoy senior status. In these circumstances, his ability to persuade, influence and convince other members is essential. . . .'

Case 4   A Project Engineer   Here we move away from the conventional job description into work we are currently doing to discern precisely what a good project engineer does, how he acts. We have interviewed all our project engineers using a technique which exhibits very clearly what they do and the relative importance attached to their (very) various activities. The most frequent classes of activity are: handling people; monitoring and progressing; cost matters; co-ordinating.

'Technical matters' rank eighth in order of frequency of mention. When these activity classes are considered in order of importance (assigned by the interviewees) the ranking is: handling people; monitoring/progressing; co-ordinating; judging/balancing (in the absence of hard data).

Thus we see very clearly from an analysis of what is actually done the importance of the collaborative process. This is also the key theme of a case study, which is now six years old, on the interfaces in the technical function. The data caused us to change the organisation to cure what it revealed, but once again emphasise the need for integration across complex interfaces.

One could go on but enough has been exposed, surely, in these examples to show that the practice of the technical specialism in a technical function is only part of the story: the exploration of the novel, problematical and potentially expensive requires the interaction of many sources of information. It is necessary that this should take place; it is essential that the interaction be conducted effectively. The motives and claims of the teachers of human relations/group skills may often be suspect, their origins, frequently in psycho-therapy, encourage caution, but it is no accident that in the development of large organisations under pressure there is a high degree of technical function interdependence which has to be facilitated by skills not built into technical specialisms. And these include the political skills of perception and reconciliation of differences. One bit of research into organisations suggests that effective modes of conflict-resolution between different functions is the universal characteristic of successful firms. Indeed, turning to the wider picture of the operation of British Industry as a whole, a very convincing case could be made for a much more intensive study of modes of conflict resolution and there is no doubt that there is much to be learnt from the political arena: without going into detail, one can discern the pressing need for a clearer understanding of negotiating processes, both as they apply to business strategy and to the relationships within the plurality of groups comprising a large scale enterprise.

To gather the threads together so far: we begin to see two main 'management science' elements emerge which directly serve the technical specialist: the first is all the corporate planning, forecasting techniques – statistical prediction, probability theory, risk and sensitivity analysis, the second, a body of knowledge around the organisation of a complex net of people and resources. This latter embraces at one pole the techniques like critical path scheduling, at the other theories of group cohesion and synergy, bridged by a cluster of topics, which for convenience can be labelled 'organisational design'.

To these must be added a third: the complex interdependence of the plants and market has called forth very sophisticated computer techniques both for optimising the operation of the complex and of single plants by the computer control of the plants themselves. These require a combination of sophisticated programming and detailed understanding of the technology, as well as of commercial variables, and really mark a revolution in our approach to running the business.

Is this a vindication for the 'management science' school? Not entirely.

In the author's firm, one is dealing in huge sums of money and potentially vicious risks to the health of the organisation. Because of the economies of scale, and the high and continually rising costs of capital investment, major capital increments are spaced in time – they are vast quantum jumps in capital employed. It cannot be surprising, therefore, that highly qualified, very intelligent and experienced people use every viable technique as a protection against disaster and the best assurance of prosperity: even so, these are aids to judgement, and the ultimate decisions do not rest on computer print outs, however sophisticated, but on a balance struck between all the elements which can, and do, affect our business.

The introductory remarks stressed the variety of industry: perhaps some of the disillusionment about, say, the Business School contribution springs from a lack of appreciation of the factors which restrict the application of 'management science'. The examples quoted above have worked because the techniques match our business needs, but one could quote many examples where time and effort has been wasted through ill-judged attempts to apply techniques which had little to offer.

It is perhaps this uncritical approach to 'management science' which has contributed to some of the failures we have experienced: there is, however, another factor. Too often – particularly in the field of applied psychology and sociology – sweeping claims have been made for the organisational benefits to be obtained from training, 'cultural change' programmes and so on. Few of these claims seem to have been substantiated, and it is fair to observe that the hypotheses underlying many of these programmes rest on very shaky foundations. The supporting research and experimentation is often very limited, and frequently based on group behaviour which bears little relation to groups and assemblies within industry.

There is a great need to understand better the interaction of individuals, groups, organisational structure and social and business environments, and it is a pity that we have perhaps gone down the wrong track. It is a fact that there is a growing volume of well founded, well researched work in this area much of it carried out in Britain. For some reason this work has been somewhat neglected, possibly because on the whole it does not offer instant panaceas. Some examples may help: in about 1962 Rowe of Edinburgh University looked at about 1400 assessments (annual staff appraisals) over a period of years. She found to my recollection, that: managers did not like doing assessments; training therein recommended was rarely executed; promotions made bore no resemblance to promotions recommended.

This finding, replicated annually in everyone's experience, has had little apparent effect on systems of staff appraisal. But at least it was genuine management science – the attempt to derive valid generalisations from observation of industrial phenomena rather than, say, the responses of psychology students in artificial situations.

Another example of considerable interest to anyone in the man management business, which most managers are, is that of Sayles, who analysed the dispute behaviour of groups, and derived a typology of behaviour characterised by the nature of their work: again, an example of generalisation from observed industrial phenomena, which seems to have had little impact.

There are other examples, such as Woodward's study of the effect of technology on organisation, Burns and Stalker's study of diversification: more recently, Stewart's study on what managers actually do. This last piece of work has proved a very valuable stimulus to our own senior managers, who find the concepts meaningful and applicable to their own experience.

To be fair, one has to add that in the author's experience, much research work is degraded and greatly oversimplified for popular consumption. One has only to think of the work of Maslow, Herzberg and McGregor (even Cyert and Marsh) which was plagiarised and popularised with very little reference to the caveats and questions clearly indicated by the original research, which recognized clearly the limitations of the experimental method, the cultural constraints and so on: the tragedy is that much good work (like the studies mentioned above) becomes tarred with the same brush, and hence we tend to write off the very real potential contribution of organisational theory to the conduct of business.

Summary

To return to the definition of management science given at the start of this paper – 'a corpus of knowledge which can be applied to the organisation and performance of an enterprise': the examples quoted make the point that the real benefit of management science is mostly to be found in that it encourages us to ask the right questions, and so helps us to work our way through an enormous array of variables with great inherent uncertainties. Further, a point which is often overlooked is that management science does at least foster the habit of making assumptions explicit, and so open to challenge – too often, debate is carried forward on the basis of implicit assumptions which often rest on very dubious interpretation of data.

This paper has ranged very widely, and there are many topics which deserve further elaboration, but it is to be hoped that it will strike some chords with all the interests represented at the conference – industrialists, educators, representatives of Government.

To summarise: the technical manager – in the petrochemical industry, at least – needs to be highly competent in his own discipline. There is no doubt that management science does help him in his managerial task, notably in the forecasting and resource management aspects of his job. Increasingly, the organisation theory and related human science topics are beginning to be helpful in so far as they are based on observation of what actually happens in industry.

The last point is one which above all else could bring new life to the business education and management science scene: if our teaching is based on good research, actual behaviour and performance and if, further, it recognises the great diversity of industry and the changing nature of the business and social environment, it can make a real contribution to performance and productivity. Implicit in all this is much better dialogue between government, industry and education, and the Conference could well be a major step in the right direction.

References

Beer S, *Brain of the Firm,* Allen Lane, 1972

Burns T and Stalker G M, *The Management of Innovation,* Tavistock, 1961

Rowe K, 'An appraisal of appraisals', *Journal of Management Studies,* Vol 1, No 1, 1964

Sayles L R, *The Behaviour of Industrial Work Groups,* Wiley, 1956

Stewart R, *Contrasts in Management,* McGraw-Hill, 1976

Woodward J, *Industrial Organisation: Theory and Practice,* OUP, 1965

The nature of management work: the commercial functions

Leslie W Rodger
HERIOT-WATT UNIVERSITY

The author is professor of business organisation at
Heriot-Watt University

The purpose of this paper is to review the development and present status of the commercial functions in a manufacturing unit.

It traces the impact which the 'marketing' concept has had on the nature of, and the management and operational responsibilities for the performance of the commercial functions. In particular it looks at the contribution that marketing has made to the development of management science, describes the work of marketing management and the knowledge and skill requirements of the modern marketing man. Finally, it points up some of the difficulties of educating and training the professional marketing men and women of the future.

Functions as means of achieving objectives

What are the commercial functions in a business enterprise? A function is a doing process. It may involve policy making, objective setting, and planning as well as putting into effect, monitoring and evaluating results. Sometimes these are the responsibility of one man or a group of people or a department; sometimes the function is split into sub-functions carried out by different people or departments. But all functions have one thing in common – a responsibility for doing something. We shall have occasion to return to this distinction between the 'doing process' as opposed to the 'thinking process' when we come to consider the marketing concept and the executive marketing function.

For the moment we will concentrate on the 'doing process'. We 'do' nothing except to achieve a desired end or objective. So that a commercial function is the organisation of activities and resources to achieve the commercial objective(s) of the business.

This paper contends that the primary commercial objective of a business, any business, is competitive effectiveness in its chosen field. Commercial functions are those functions in the business enterprise concerned with the competitive effectiveness of the firm's operations in the market-place, and this effectiveness is measured in terms of market response and judged in terms of commercial results: sales and profit.

From one point of view, it can be argued that the only thing that a business generates internally are costs; a business enterprise is essentially a cost centre. The market is the only place where profit can be made. Even where one firm sells its output, or supplies services to another firm within the same group, it would appear perfectly valid to regard the latter company as representing the market – or one market at any rate – of the supplying company. Everything that a business unit does accumulates cost – whether buying-in or selling out – right up to the point where cash receipts from actual sales flow back into the unit. Cash flow is the name of the game. The line between going bankrupt and remaining solvent can be a very fine one; as thin, indeed, as an unpaid invoice.

A manufacturing unit buys facilities and inputs – buildings, labour, machinery, raw materials, semi-processed goods and components. Whenever a firm's own products – whether they be work-in-progress, or finished goods – stop moving for any reason on their journey towards the intermediate customer (who may be a processor, converter or distributor) and on towards the final user or consumer, they accumulate cost . . . the cost of warehousing and storage, carriage and delivery, insurance, stock-handling, order-processing and packing, stock obsolescence and deterioration, and working capital tied-up in unsaleable or slow-moving inventory.

All the manufacturing unit's efforts are converted into commercial results, that is to say, profitable sales, by satisfied customers, which is why manufacturing may properly be described as a customer-servicing and customer-problem solving process and not just a goods-producing process. In this context, competitive effectiveness means servicing the customer better than one's competitors. This means doing the better thing by the customer – identifying, anticipating and developing the better product and service packages, determining the better pricing, promotion and distribution policies in relation to the market's existing and emerging requirements. First and foremost, a manufacturing unit has to be organised to be competitively effective in terms of being in the right markets with the right products and services to sell at the time the customer wants them and at a price which the market can absorb – and yielding a worthwhile profit to the unit. These are the proper concerns of the commercial function(s) within the manufacturing unit.

Marketing as the focus of commercial functions

There is nothing new about these commercial functions. Some one, or some group, within the manufacturing unit has always been responsible for product planning and selection, pricing, selling, promotion and distribution. But it has not always been the overall responsibility of one individual or group. It has not been uncommon in the past for product planning and selection to be the responsibility of the production or engineering department, and for promotion and distribution to be the responsibility of the sales department. There was not necessarily any co-ordination between the two beyond the understanding that it was the job of the sales department to dispose, as profitability as it could, of the goods churned out by the production department without having any or much of a say in what products ought to be produced. In this sense, a manufacturing unit was said to be 'production-oriented'.

The so-called 'marketing approach' looks first at what the consumer wants, develops the most effective 'marketing mix' (the most appropriate product/service/price/promotion/distribution combination), and gears up the production unit accordingly. Manufacturing units adopting this 'marketing orientation' bring together the traditional commercial functions described above under a single management which may be represented at board level by a marketing director or commercial director. Co-ordination and integration of the elements of the marketing mix are thereby made easier.

This is the theory. In practical application there are wide variations, particularly as between industrial product manufacturing units and consumer product manufacturing units. In the case of the former it is not at all uncommon to find a marketing services department providing promotional services (advertising, public relations, technical literature, exhibitions, etc) and economic intelligence and market research services to divisional general managers and corporate management. The management and control of the field selling function, especially with highly technical products, and the pricing function may report separately to the divisional or product group general manager who himself acts as the focal point for marketing co-ordination. The organisational solution to the problem of technical–commercial co-ordination has been found with varying degrees of effectiveness by:

(a) product manager systems focusing on the management of a specific product or group of products selling to a variety of market outlets;

(b) market manager systems focusing on the management of a specific market or group of markets for the firm's complete range of products; and

(c) technical-commercial manager systems focusing on plant and product scheduling to meet sales requirements.

There is little difference in principle between industrial and consumer products marketing. The difference is rather one of emphasis in the way in which the elements of the marketing mix are blended together to meet the particular needs of customers who may be a few specialised purchasers or a mass of consumers. The basic distinction lies in the purpose for which the goods are bought; goods bought for organisational purposes rather than for personal or family consumption. Certain goods can, of course, be bought for both purposes: typewriters, electronic calculators, motor cars. The balance of marketing activities can be very similar in certain situations and quite different in others. As was said at the beginning of this section, executive responsibility for the commercial functions has always resided somewhere within the manufacturing unit regardless of its size and degree of management specialisation. Someone has always had to decide what to make, at what price to the customer, how to promote what is to be offered to the customer and how physically to get it to the customer's premises. What we have been describing is the executive commercial function, the 'doing' process.

What is new is the developing underlying philosophy behind the whole business operation, and in this regard marketing has contributed more than just an organisational mode or a battery of specialised, sophisticated techniques in market research, sales forecasting, promotion, distribution and after-sales service.

It is necessary at this point to distinguish between marketing as a concept or management perspective towards the running of a manufacturing unit and marketing as a technology, or group of specialised activities which certain executives within the unit carry out. We must distinguish between marketing as a strategic 'thinking' process and marketing as tactical 'doing' process which is concerned with the way the marketing mix is put together and deployed in the market place.

Marketing's prime contribution to management philosophy has been to put the customer, if not at the very centre of the manufacturing unit's planning activities, then at least in very much closer proximity to the managing nerve centre of the unit.

Marketing must start as a concept which defines the purpose of manufacturing operations rather than as a description of operations themselves. And that purpose is seen to be the identification, creation and delivery of optimum customer values, ie maximum values at minimum costs, at a profit. The words 'at a profit' are crucial. It is no part of a manufacturing unit's purpose to create satisfied customers at any cost. To survive and grow a manufacturing unit must earn a satisfactory profit if it is to continue to serve its customers on a long-term basis and if it is to fulfil its obligations to its employees, shareholders, suppliers, the local community and society at large. Marketing, as Levitt has said, 'is a consolidating view of the business process'. Everyone is involved to some degree in creating value for the customer or in minimising the delivered cost of the product. It is a view which concerns everybody in the manufacturing unit from the shop floor to the boardroom, from the works director to the telephone exchange operator and the person sitting at the reception desk in the front hall. It aims at encouraging everyone to consider their individual tasks with the interests of the customer in mind and in the light of the impact that their decisions and actions can have on the customer. It seeks to eliminate the distinction between those in the company who serve the customer and those who think they don't or that it doesn't matter.

The executive marketing function is essentially a matching process. It is concerned with the profitable matching of the manufacturing unit's capabilities with the requirements of the customer. This matching is achieved by structuring the whole unit around the perceived requirements of the customer (the 'marketing concept') through the planning, co-ordination and control of the product/service offered, the price that is charged, the style and weight of selling and promotion and the way in which it is delivered, regardless of whether this is done by a formalised marketing department headed by a marketing director at board level or by a group of individuals without a marketing title between them.

The mere existence of a so-called 'marketing director' or of a specialist marketing department is no guarantee that the marketing concept is really established or that the specific marketing function is being carried out effectively at the operational level. What matters is what lies behind the titles of the personnel involved, what it is that they actually do and what their basic philosophy and motivation is for doing it.

It is the recognition and acceptance of the need to plan ahead the 'best' match between the manufacturing unit's capabilities and the particular customers' requirements which the unit seeks to serve that calls for the formalisation of marketing as a specific function within the unit and determines the precise form that it takes.

What has marketing science brought to the commercial functions?

Marketing science has provided management with a range of diagnostic and analytic tools or techniques to help bring about a more effective match of the manufacturing unit's capabilities to market opportunities. Marketing has borrowed and adapted methods and tools from other scientific disciplines, the behavioural sciences, mathematics, statistics, as well as from technology, such as electronics, computers. It has freely adapted operational research methods to the solution of marketing problems as, for example, in the application of queuing theory to customer servicing problems, in the application of network analysis to new product development and product launch programmes, and in the application of linear (and non-linear) programming to problems of determining the most profitable combination of products to be made from limited resources, the optimum location of warehouses and depots, optimum stock levels to meet sales requirements at minimum cost, the planning of salesmen's journeys and calling cycles.

It has been in the forefront of developments in applying probability analysis to the investigation of buyer behaviour and in the construction of mathematical models and communication models. It has applied statistical methods of time series analysis, trend analysis, correlation and regression analysis to sales forecasting and, for purposes of market research, it has developed sampling techniques to a fine art.

Perhaps more important than the application of a specific technique to a particular problem, has been the scientific methodology which marketing has brought to bear on business problems. Marketing was perhaps the first field in which management by objectives was practised to any major extent. Objective setting is a pre-requisite to marketing strategic planning and both require a strong information base provided by economic intelligence and marketing research. The quantity and quality of the information made available to management for the purposes of setting objectives, determining strategy and preparing business plans is perhaps the most significant contribution that the marketing approach has brought to the manufacturing unit.

As precursor to present-day corporate planning, marketing planning operated on a different time-scale. The marketing plan started out essentially as a year by year exercise. As management's time horizons and perspectives lengthened due to longer run pressures for change and the need to plan for five years ahead or more, they began developing corporate plans with, of course, a strong marketing input. Strictly speaking the marketing plan should be a by-product of the overall corporate plan and this is now probably becoming the norm. In so far as the marketing plan is concerned with implementing those aspects of the corporate plan which relate to the manufacturing unit's activities in the market-place on a year by year basis, it seems clear that marketing considerations must weigh heavily in the development of the corporate plan.

To get back to the marketing approach. Its bedrock is information about markets at home and abroad; about what the customer requires and how well his requirements are being met by competitors; about buyer behaviour patterns; about distribution channel habits, attitudes and requirements; about the effectiveness of alternative methods of communicating with customers and of alternative promotional programmes.

The marketing imperative has also created an awareness of the importance of hitherto comparatively neglected areas of business operations. Pricing, for example, is a marketing tool which is still too infrequently practised consciously as a positive element in commercial strategy. According to Wilson, 'The study of pricing techniques and pricing strategies has unquestionably produced much new and important evidence on the potency of pricing both as a tool and as a weapon in the competitive world within which all industrial firms operate' (Atkin and Skinner, 1975).

In the area of distribution, which we take to mean the whole process of getting the product to the customer, marketing management cannot take the view that this is the concern of others. For in so far as marketing is concerned with the creation and delivery of optimum customer values at a profit it has a vital interest in the process which adds time and place value to the product (without which it is worthless) and minimises the cost of delivery to the customer.

According to Christopher and his co-authors, there has been a tendency in many manufacturing units to treat distribution as something of a necessary, but mechanical, activity that incurs costs and is something to do with transport. Too few companies have seen their physical distribution and materials management efforts as potentially contributing in a vital and positive way to profitability. However, if the marketing department is judged for performance in terms of sales and market shares there will be a tendency to push the costs of distribution into someone else's cost centre. The problems caused by the compartmentalisation of the manufacturing unit into a series of discrete activities has given rise to the 'logistics concept'.

From the same report:

'The emphasis behind the logistics concept is on systems. It suggests that the *movement* activity in a company is so wide-reaching and pervasive in its impacts that is should be considered as a total system. Thus instead of marketing, production, distribution, purchasing, etc, all working away oblivious of the others and attempting to optimise their own activity, the logistics concept suggests that it may be necessary for some, or all, of these areas to operate sub-optimally in order that the whole system may be more effective. So, for example, the marketing manager must be prepared if necessary to accept a lower level of service than he would like; or the production manager must be prepared to schedule shorter runs with more changes, if the overall effectiveness of the system is to be maximised.

'To move this concept from the realms of theory to those of practice involves a consideration of the areas of concern to logistics management. There are five key decision areas that together constitute the logistics mix:

Facility decisions
Inventory decisions
Communications decisions
Unitisation decisions
Transport decisions.

'Together these five areas constitute the total costs of distribution within a company. Further, however, it is frequently the case that a decision taken in one area will have an effect on the other four areas. Thus a decision to close a depot, a facility decision, will affect the transport costs, the inventory allocation and perhaps data processing costs – this is the idea of a cost trade-off. Managing the logistics function involves a continuous search for such trade-offs, the intention being to secure a reduction in total costs by changing the cost structure in one area.

'The important feature of this logistics mix concept is that transport is seen as being just one element amongst five. Conventionally in many companies transport is distribution; yet viewed in this total sense it may be that it accounts for only a small proportion of total logistics costs.

'One of the major problems of conventional approaches to distribution is that responsibility for it is spread over many discrete functional areas. It has already been suggested that a too-heavy emphasis on compartmentalisation in the company leads to a sub-optimal situation overall. In one Swiss engineering company responsibility for stock levels throughout the system was in the hands of the production department; yet at the same time the purchasing manager was pursuing policies which conflicted with production policy, the distribution manager operated an inflexible delivery system and the marketing manager was driven to despair with the erratic service levels that resulted. All this resulted from a failure to take a systems-approach to the logistics function within the company.

'The acceptance of the integrative systems-based approach that characterises the logistics concept implies a recognition that there is an inter-relationship between the parts of the whole of such a nature that action affecting one part can well affect all others. Any action taken must therefore be considered in the light of its effect on all parts of the business and on the overriding objectives of the company. Thus the company can be viewed as a number of interlinked subsystems which must somehow be united if overall effectiveness is to be maximised. The distribution planner under such an orientation must be concerned with the flow of materials through the whole business process, from raw materials through to the finished goods arriving at the customer's premises.

'Thus, while physical distribution management is concerned only with those flows from the end of the production line to the consumer, the integrated approach of logistics encompasses the total flow of materials and related information into, through, and out of the corporate system.'

In drawing attention to these matters, marketing management has helped towards a better understanding of industrial dynamics. It has at the same time demolished any argument for a marketing takeover of the business.

The role of marketing management within the manufacturing unit

A systems approach to business operations highlights the dangers that can arise where any one of the specific business functions – engineering, production, marketing or finance – seeks to take over the running of the manufacturing unit. Most specialists tend to believe that their particular activity is the crux of the business.

General management, for ever in search of the philosopher's stone which can turn base products into gold, has turned with faith, hope but little charity to new concepts and techniques which would automatically solve management's problems. Marketing was one of these.

The marketing fraternity who, as you would expect, are adept at selling themselves and their ideas, have perhaps been guilty of over-stating their case; and general management, for a time, has been guilty of letting them do so. While the marketing concept may be a consolidating view of the business process and a major factor in corporate planning, this is not the same thing as saying that marketing is top dog or must always call the company tune.

In practice, marketing men have had to shed their misplaced zeal in their own abilities to plan, co-ordinate and control their manufacturing unit's entire future. Marketing executive management is not general management any more than production management is, or financial management. The marketing executive function is, or should be, part of an integrated stream of research–development–design–engineering–manufacturing–selling–financial activity in which no single discipline or specialist function has primacy over the others. The proper instrument for achieving the necessary planning, integration and control is not an all-powerful marketing department or marketing supremo, but a closely-knit top management executive group in which these major functions are represented and which can take a consolidating (marketing) view of the business.

It is this group's task to build bridges between the different functions, to avoid or sort out the inter-departmental conflicts which will inevitably arise, so as to create a balance of organisation and effort from which everybody, or as many people as possible, will gain – the manu-facturing unit itself, its customers, its employees, shareholders, suppliers, the local community and society as a whole.

The essence of good marketing is team effort. It is precisely because marketing affects so much of the manufacturing unit's resources and activities and because marketing plans require the support of massive investments in production plant, materials and logistical services that the marketing group within the unit has a special obligation and responsibility to make the integrative mode of management work.

Nowhere, perhaps, is the need to establish direct linkages more important than at the R&D–marketing interface. The limited research that has been carried out to date indicates that the failure of many manufacturing units to exploit the fruits of the R&D capability is a consequence of its divorce from marketing, particularly from market research into user needs. The failure would appear to be two-way. Marketing management has steered clear of involvement in the research and development process, possibly because of the former's historical non-technical pedigree. R&D management has not understood the marketing function or its potential contribution to successful innovation, possibly because of its traditional non-commercial pedigree.

It is easy enough to conjecture that what is needed is more interchange of roles at the R&D-marketing interface, that a new hybrid technical and innovation management needs to be developed by encouraging science and engineering graduates into industrial management covering prototype work, production and marketing as opposed to pure research and development.

It seems likely, however, that more research into the interface relationship over a period of time will be necessary to understand the processes at work. In particular, an action research programme in a sample of manufacturing units with interface management problems which would attempt to implement change, by agreement, and observe the process of change *in situ,* would appear to offer the best means of advancing our knowledge in this vital area.

The Institute of Marketing has described the marketing management job in the following terms: 'If we may look upon the Managing Director as equivalent to the captain of a ship, then it is the Marketing Director, or senior marketing executive, who represents the Navigator. His is the responsibility to provide the Captain with all the necessary information and guidance to make a safe and successful landfall. In the same way, the marketing executive is responsible for providing the basic information and guidance about prospective markets, their behaviour, size and potential for each product and service within the company'.

Marketing research, product development, marketing planning, communications planning and co-ordination, selling and sales management, sales training and sales forecasting are broadly the activities of the marketing man.

The work in a consumer goods' manufacturing unit   In the case of packaged goods the marketing process falls into a number of distinct phases as illustrated in Figure 3.1.

(a) Studying the market to find out what the customer wants, what alternative products are already available to him or her, and to identify a selling opportunity for the company.
(b) Planning the product/service/price/profit combination guided by market research data and with the aid of technical research and development.

Figure 3.1   The marketing process

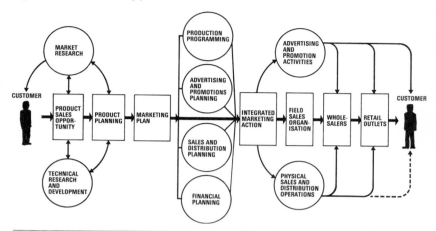

Source: *Marketing in A Competitive Economy*, Leslie W Rodger, Associated Business Programmes, Fourth Edition, 1974

(c) Preparing the marketing plan incorporating:
   (1) production programme;
   (2) communications (advertising and promotions) plan;
   (3) sales, merchandising, and physical distribution plans;
   (4) financial plans.

(d) Co-ordinating and integrating marketing action through the field sales organisation to distributors, eg wholesalers and retailers, through communications media, through physical sales, merchandising, and distribution operations.

(e) Monitoring the consumer market, evaluating the results of the company's efforts and feed-back to the marketing planning centre as a basis for the next planning cycle.

The work in an industrial products' manufacturing unit   60 per cent of Britain's largest companies are engaged in marketing industrial products in which goods are sold to buyers in other companies for organisational purposes or incorporation in their own products, as opposed to sales to retailers and to consumers. There are at least seven different types of industrial products or services:

(a) Raw materials – coal, iron ore, wool, cocoa, oils, fat, etc.
(b) Components – fasteners, springs, rivets, condensers, integrated circuits, TV tubes, etc.

(c) Consumables – acids, paints, varnishes, lubricants, adhesives, etc.

(d) Packaging and wrapping materials – paper, cardboard, plastics, plywood, cans, etc.

(e) Plant and equipment – cranes, engines, presses, computers, etc.

(f) Technical Services – communications equipment, design services, surveying services, etc.

(g) General Services – catering, laundry, telephone cleaning, etc.

Almost all selling involves face-to-face interviews with prospective customers. What particularly distinguishes the selling of industrial products from that of consumer goods, is the precise nature of these interviews and the technical demands made on the salesmen. Industrial salesmen have to deal with expert buyers and typically more than one individual within the buying company will influence the purchasing decision. To sell capital equipment the salesmen may face long hours of negotiations possibly spread over many months, sometimes years. Often it will not be a question of selling a standard product but of agreeing a specification which incorporates the buyer's approach to a particular technical problem. The salesmen must be aware of the effect of design decisions on profitability. Planning, too, will be important for a project may run into years and involve complex financial and contractual obligations. In such cases, the salesman must be a skilled development engineer.

What the modern marketing man needs to know   He needs to know something about the techniques of marketing research, since everything stems from an understanding of the customer, his requirements and his problems. The marketer's success will depend on understanding and anticipating these requirements and problems more accurately than, and coming up with better solutions than, his competitors.

He must be knowledgeable about distribution channels; about the habits, attitudes and requirements of agents, wholesalers, and retailers, who must be persuaded to handle and actively support the product before it can reach the customer.

He must understand the psychology and techniques of face-to-face selling – even if he is no great shakes at it himself. The manufacturing unit's sales force is the main instrument through which he must work in getting the product into key distributors or directly into the hands of the customer.

He must appreciate the part that advertising, sales promotion, exhibitions, technical seminars, merchandising and packaging design can play in product presentation.

Although he need not be an expert in production he must know enough about the potentialities and limitations of the manufacturing process to be aware of the effects of design and engineering decisions on the profitable utilisation of plant and to persuade his production colleagues that modifications in the product required to solve customers' technical problems are not entirely out of the question. He needs to be highly literate and numerate; the former to be able to present a case to his own board colleagues and line managers, to the customers' board of directors or other key groups who are important to the business, using all manner of audio and visual aids; and the latter because a significant part of marketing work is statistical in nature and increasingly requires the aid of a computer.

To quote Edward Nixon, Managing Director of IBM United Kingdom Limited and Chairman of the CBI Committee on Marketing and Consumer Affairs.

'The marketing man emerges as a rather particular kind of businessman or executive, broad in outlook and necessarily highly trained by education and experience to use a large armoury of marketing techniques. The outcome of great undertakings in production and distribution depends upon his ability and imagination; his plans require the support of massive investment in productive plant and materials and in costly forms of communication such as advertising and sales force operation. Only those who combine the right personal qualities with a completely professional approach both in preparation for, and in the execution of, the marketing management role are likely to be entrusted with its substantial responsibilities.'

In summary, a proper and recognised level of education in marketing, coupled with sound practical experience, must be the route for the professional marketing man of the future.

It is probably generally agreed that specialised marketing education is something that preferably should be acquired after some experience in industry. This can and does create real problems for both employers and employees, Employers, on the one hand, must be prepared to release their most promising executives on sponsorship to undertake recognised graduate-level or postgraduate courses of study and many employees have to be prepared to accept some financial sacrifice in the short term in order to pursue a course of study in marketing. It may be that we will have to follow the American pattern in accepting more direct entries from universities into our postgraduate business schools.

Whilst one can agree that the educational experience might be more valuable and helpful to the student if it is acquired after some acquaintance with industry or commerce, this is not to say that courses of business and marketing studies taken in the polytechnics and universities before any industrial experience is obtained are without value.

The more post-experience students the better. Although our present higher education system is geared to school-leavers, there is no doubt that a significant switch of emphasis towards the post-experience candidate is likely in the not too distant future.

All efforts by industry to surmount these difficulties are more than welcome. But if industry in the short term wants more graduate managers, whose education by and large cannot be funded by industry, and if vocationally-oriented sixth-form studies are not going to be provided by schools on anything like the scale necessary, then it must make the best use it can of the young people who go on to the universities and polytechnics. A flow of literate and numerate graduates with an understanding of basic business processes and business organisation is not a resource that should be lightly discarded in favour of the school leaver who can then be trained up on-the-job and later sent on approved courses of study at the company's expense.

Atkin B and Skinner R, *How British Industry Prices,* Industrial Market Research Limited, 1975.

Burns T M and Stalker G M, *The Management of Innovation,* Tavistock, 1961.

Central Advisory Council for Science and Technology, *Technological Innovation in Britain,* HMSO, 1968.

Centre for the Study of Industrial Innovation, *On the Shelf,* 1971.

Christopher M, Walters D and Wills G, *Introduction to Marketing: The Cranfield Approach,* MCB Books, 1975.

Levitt T, *The Marketing Mode: Pathways to Corporate Growth,* McGraw-Hill, 1970.

Science Policy Research Unit, *Success and Failure in Industrial Innovation (Project Sappho),* University of Sussex, 1972.

Thomas M and Goodwin J, 'An Examination of the Management of the R and D – Marketing Interface in Several British Companies', *Quarterly Review of Marketing,* Autumn 1976.

Way Sir R, *The Way Report – Machine Tool Industry,* HMSO, 1970.

The 'non-productive' component within the productive sector: a problem of management control

John Child
UNIVERSITY OF ASTON

The author is professor of organisational behaviour at the University of Aston. He would like to thank members of the Central Personnel Division of Dunlop for making available the employment statistics cited, especially Roland Sparkes and Peter Melville. He is also grateful to Dr Zvi Maimon and Professor Janet Schriesheim for their comments on a draft of the paper

The problem

In the last year or so, the view has often been taken that the regeneration of manufacturing industry is a necessary condition for improvement in Britain's economic condition. Tony Benn, for example, has consistently argued that the imbalance in the economy could be corrected by curtailing service activity and investing heavily via the National Enterprise Board in manufacturing industry so as to substitute manufactured products for home and export. The commercial service sector has been symbolised by the parasitical property developer, and contrasted unfavourably with 'productive' industry. Many have asked anxiously how our best university graduates can be attracted into manufacturing, particularly engineering.

One of the most important contributions which Bacon and Eltis have made in their book, *Britain's Economic Problem: Too Few Producers*, is to refine this oversimplified view that manufacturing industry is coincidental with productive industry. Instead of dividing economic activities into those which are manufacturing (or industrial) and those which are not, they argue for a distinction between activities which produce marketed outputs that can be sold for an economic return and those which do not. Private-sector services fall into the marketed sector. Bacon and Eltis point out that the total private consumption, investment and export needs of the country have to be supplied from the marketed output of both manufacturing and services. These should therefore be regarded as productive industry in contrast to other activities – those in government, public service and the loss-making corporations sustained by public subsidy.

Bacon and Eltis express concern at the fact that there has been a long-term shift of expenditure and employment to the non-productive sector. In 1961 the entitlement to buy marketed output by those who did not produce it was 41.5 per cent before tax; by 1974 this had risen to 60.5 per cent. Over the same period, employment in the market sector declined by 5 per cent, while that in the non-productive sector rose by 45 per cent. In June 1961, employment in the non-market sector stood at 3 019 000, representing 16.1 per cent of the market sector. In June 1976, it was 4 720 000 representing 27.3 per cent of the market sector, and still rising.

Two qualifications need to be added to Bacon and Eltis's analysis, the second of which will be the concern of this paper. First, they tend to ignore the fact that some public services are potentially marketable, and would almost certainly pay for themselves if this were permitted. Roads could be run on a toll basis; if there were no 'free' alternative, people would pay for services such as education and medicine, as indeed some still do. No one would seriously suggest that the productive sector of the economy could function adequately in the absence of such services. The really unproductive sector centres on administration, which can be counted almost as pure overhead. In a more recent article for the *Sunday Times,* Bacon and Eltis began to recognise this distinction by commenting that, with employment in public administration continuing to rise between March and June 1976 and that in education and health faltering, 'those most directly concerned with producing the social wage were starting to cut back while employment in administration was increasing faster than before'.

The second qualification argues for a refinement of the distinction between producers and non-producers within sectors as well as between them. It is built upon a concern that the phenomenon noted for the public sector in the preceding quotation also applies within the sector that Bacon and Eltis have distinguished as productive. In other words, (1) within the productive sector not all employment is equally productive, and (2) downturns in activity are accompanied by a more severe cutback in productive employment than in the less productive component. If this is the case, then not only will resources have been shifting from productive to non-productive sectors, but also from productive to non-productive components within the productive sector.

In most industrial economies a long-term increase in the percentage of 'administrative, technical and clerical' employees within the occupational population is a now well-established trend. It is not apparent from overall national figures how much this represents a shift in the balance of employment between sectors as opposed to within sectors. C Northcote Parkinson was perhaps the first to illustrate the shift away from direct employment and towards non-productive 'administrative proliferation' within a sector, albeit in this case the public sector itself. Appendix 1 reproduces a table from his *Law of Delay,* extending data first provided in his famous *Parkinson's Law* and clearly demonstrating the phenomenon at work. Much of the criticism which has been directed at recent trends in the civil service, and in local government and the National Health Service since their 1974 re-organisations, is sustained by the fear that an expansion of their staffs does not so much represent additional direct work in service provided as an inflation of the non-direct component. The question then arises whether such inflation is a general organisational phenomenon, which might extend to the productive sector. If the non-productive component is increasing within the productive sector this represents a further charge on the return from marketable activities.

For many years the great majority of studies into the relative size of the indirect or administrative component in organisations concluded that this diminished as overall size of organisation increased (Child, 1973b). Since the natural tendency has been for organisations to grow over time, and for the average size of organisations to increase, the comforting conclusion could be drawn that there was not a serious problem of growing non-productive overhead. Unfortunately, virtually all of this research is practically worthless because we now appreciate that it suffered from basic methodological problems concerning in particular the correlation of ratios with their denominators and the use of cross-sectional data to impute dynamic longitudinal processes. Basically, what is required are studies which examine movements in the absolute numbers of people employed in different categories over relatively long periods of time that include phases of growing and declining activity.

Only a few such studies have been published so far and these are not of industrial companies. They are, however, quite revealing. Hendershot and James found among American school districts that those which had grown rapidly showed decreases in the proportion of administrative to direct staff, while those which had grown slowly tended to show increases in the proportion of administrative staff. Freeman and Hannan studied 769 Californian school districts over the period 1968 to 1972. They found that in growing districts, administrative staffs increased roughly in proportion to the numbers of direct employees. In declining districts, however, the loss of direct employees was not matched by a loss of administrative personnel. The indirect component as a whole – administrators and other non-direct staff – tended to increase on the upswings but to decrease less on the downswings. An earlier study by Tsouderos also found in ten American voluntary associations whose membership had risen and then declined, that the numbers of administrative employees actually continued to rise for some time even when total size declined. Does this type of process operate for non-direct employees within manuacturing industry and if so, what are its effects over a long period of time?

I was fortunate enough to be given access to statistics for United Kingdom employment in the Dunlop Group over the period from end-March 1948 to end-June 1977. These statistics were collected on a quarterly basis by the company up to the end of 1972 and on a half-yearly basis since, giving a total of 109 readings. At this stage, data are available on total employment, broken down into male and female operatives, male and female staff. Apart from the inclusion of plant maintenance workers in the 'operative' category, the breakdown between operative and staff is equivalent to one between direct and indirect employees. A close examination of these statistics reveals trends which are remarkably consistent with the American studies just cited. In my opinion, there is reason to believe that similar trends would be found within many, if not most, other British manufacturing companies, and one should not, therefore, make any special evaluation of Dunlop on the basis of these figures.

Figure 4.1 shows the movements of total operative employment (unbroken line) and total staff employment (broken line) over the period end-March 1948 to end-June 1977. Operative employment stood at 24 828 in the first period and at 25 972 by the close – an overall increase of 4.61 per cent. Staff employment commenced at 8 672 and closed in mid-1977 at 17 745 – an overall increase of 104.62 per cent. What makes Dunlop's case more interesting is that the company experienced a period of falling profitability and retrenchment after 1969, and that it had also experienced earlier ups and downs. It is therefore possible to examine the trend of employment in direct and indirect categories during phases of growth and cutback.

Figure 4.1 indicates that during periods of growth there were rises in both direct and indirect employment. However, with the exception of the last major downturn, whenever direct employment was cut back staff numbers actually continued to rise albeit at a much reduced rate of increase. Table 4.1 lists the percentage changes in the two categories of employment over thirteen time periods comprising seven upswings (A–B, C–D, E–F, G–H, I–J, K–L, M–N) and six downswings (B–C, D–E, F–G, H–I, J–K, L–M). On the whole, there has been a percentage increase of indirect employees accompanying that of direct employees during periods of expansion, while during five out of six periods of decline in direct employment the indirect figure has not experienced a complementary fall. Even in the last and most serious period of retrenchment, the decline in indirect employment has been proportionately less than that in direct employment.

What has been happening, within Dunlop, is a continuous increase in the proportion of indirect employment due to a kind of ratchet phenomenon. Rises in company activity jack up indirect alongside direct employment, but downturns do not let indirect numbers fall to anywhere near the same extent as direct employees. When the next upturn comes, indirect and direct employment are both jacked up again. The overall effect is a spectacular difference in the percentage growth of the two employment categories from 1948 to 1977.

Figure 4.1 shows how the degree of variation in levels of direct employment within Dunlop has been much greater than that in levels of

Figure 4.1   Dunlop Group (UK) – trends in operative and staff employment from first quarter 1948 to mid-1977

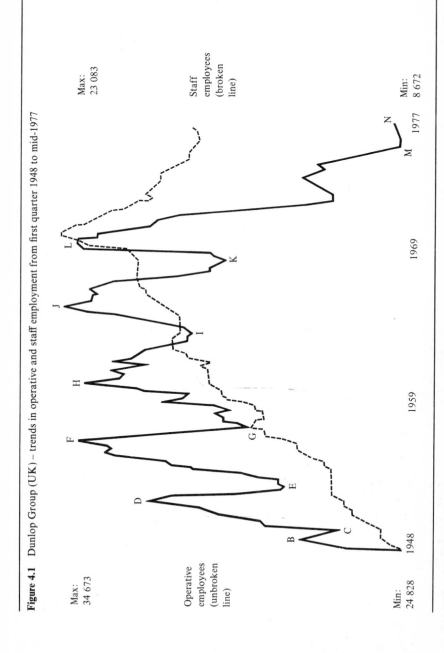

Max:
34 673

Operative
employees
(unbroken
line)

Min:
24 828

Max:
23 083

Staff
employees
(broken
line)

Min:
8 672

1948   1959   1969   1977

Table 4.1   Dunlop Group (UK) – percentage changes in operative and staff employment over selected time periods

Time period	Dates (quarter ending, year)	Percentages change in: Operatives	Staff
A–B	3/48–12/48	+12.90	+13.65
B–C	12/48–6/49	−4.07	+0.02
C–D	6/49–9/51	+20.38	+17.76
D–E	9/51–9/52	−11.97	+2.31
E–F	9/52–12/55	+20.87	+22.37
F–G	12/55–9/56	−14.49	+3.47
G–H	9/56–12/59	+15.17	+13.10
H–I	12/59–3/63	−8.27	+6.52
I–J	3/63–3/65	+11.44	+4.05
J–K	3/65–3/68	−13.06	+5.18
K–L	3/68–3/69	+14.23	+11.08
L–M	3/69–6/76	−27.07	−22.06
M–N	6/76–6/77	+3.42	+1.58

staff employment. The company has been regarding operative labour as a variable cost which can be adjusted to suit economic circumstances, while staff, up to 1969 at least, have been treated as a relatively fixed cost. Taking the period since 1948 as a whole, changes in staff numbers did not move significantly in tune with changes in profitability or value of sales, while operative numbers did. Annual percentage changes in the rate of pre-tax profit earned on capital employed have been more highly associated with annual percentage changes in total operatives ($r = 0.52$ from 28 annual readings, $p < 0.01$) than have annual percentage changes in the value of sales ($r = 0.37$ from 28 annual readings, $p < 0.05$). Adjustment in operative employment has taken place more or less in conjunction with changes in company performance since building a yearly lag into the calculation eliminates the relationships. When changes in both profitability and sales are taken into account, they predict 30.5 per cent of movements in operative employment. Even taken in combination, annual changes in profitability and sales do not appear to have had an appreciable effect on the number of staff employed. They account for 6.7 per cent of the changes in staff employment during the same year and for 9.9 per cent of changes during the following year. Neither of these relationships reaches normally acceptable levels of statistical confidence.

If this relative inflexibility of indirect employment in response to changing levels of company performance, and its rise proportional to direct employment, is found in other British companies, *prima facie* it would appear that the problem of non-producers in the economy extends both to their distribution between sectors and to their distribution within the productive sector itself. In effect, it is more serious than even Bacon and Eltis claim. The fact that Dunlop's experience is consistent with the other examples reported by researchers, despite differences in type of organisation and location, suggest that it may have been repeated many times elsewhere within the productive sector.

Justifications advanced for this phenomenon

There are a number of explanations and justifications which can be advanced for increases in indirect employment. These constitute objections to the foregoing argument and require examination. First, by no means all indirect employment in a company can legitimately be categorised as non-productive. Direct labour could not produce effectively without the support of some managerial and technical functions. The relevant questions to ask then become 'how many indirects are really necessary to support direct activities?', 'what kinds of indirects are required?', and 'what is the balance between the benefits they contribute and the costs they entail?'. In this respect it is always appropriate to evaluate the matching of needs, resources and expenditure, and to examine alternatives ways of staffing to provide the matching. How much 'specialist' work could, for example, more productively be incorporated within line management or taken over by direct employees? An efficiency criterion would require that the number of indirects be kept to as low a figure as is compatible with providing necessary services for current and future productive activity. A steady increase in their numbers has to answer to that criterion. The problem is thus in part one of exercising managerial control over the indirect component, and this raises questions of management philosophy and organisation which are considered later.

Second, a long-term increase in the proportion of indirect staff may be the price which the productive sector has to pay for the increasing scale and complexity that characterise the contemporary organisation of its activities. Large scale organisation may be felt to bring certain economic advantages in terms of lower unit production costs, diversification, market power and so forth (though this argument has, of course, been seriously challenged in recent years). In that case, a higher investment in administration often becomes necessary in order to control and integrate the potentially far less manageable giant company.

These are managerial diseconomies of scale which may nonetheless be considered a cost worth bearing, although there remains every reason to keep these administrative overheads to a minimum and under control.

Third, while the scale of organisations may generate complexity, so also does the changing context of management decision making. Companies are now involved in many more interdependent relationships with outside bodies, not least with the agencies of government. It is generally agreed that the pace of change and competition has increased. All these factors generate complexity and uncertainty. They render decision making a more elaborate process. Strategic business decisions are coming to have wider implications and require more interfunctional and specialist contributions. The size of investments involved and the rate of change in many fields also raise the opportunity costs of making a poor decision or an ill-timed one. These developments swell the amount of information that has to be taken into account, and also supplied elsewhere. More indirect staff have to be recruited to collect, evaluate and generally process the information load. These staff have to be integrated and this may require the employment of co-ordinators. The back-up required for decision making is therefore growing. The idea prevalent in government that major decision makers should constantly be exposed to different sources of intelligence, conflicting interpretations of that intelligence and contradictory recommendations for action may also be spreading to large companies. While the advisors immediately involved may be relatively few, the supporting systems behind them could be large.

A further burden of information is being imposed on companies today by government. At the conference to which this paper was first given, a finger was pointed by industrialists to the burgeoning weight of legislation and demands for information as a major source of infla- tion in indirect and commercially non-productive employment. Many companies now have departments dealing with non-productive areas such as price applications. It is not clear, however, that these legal and statistical requirements mainly of recent origin can account for many additional staff employees or that they explain why the shift towards indirect employment has gone on for so many years.

Fourth, the possibility cannot be ignored that an increase in indirect employment is a function of technical progress, which generates economies in direct employment via mechanisation and automation, and which also brings about increases in staff employment because of greater research and development activity, and relevant new techniques in financial control, forecasting, manpower management, operational research, planning and so forth. In these ways, one would expect technical progress to create some long-term proportional shift away from direct employment. What technical progress, nor indeed the other justifications for expansions in indirect staff, cannot satisfactorily explain, however, is the pattern of the movement. Why have falls and then recoveries in direct employment not been accompanied simply by consolidation in support staff rather than by further substantial increases? The fact that direct employment in Dunlop up to 1969 recovered so strongly after cutbacks implies that labour saving technical progress was not a major underlying factor, while it also seems doubtful that new management techniques can account for the spectacular rise in staff up to 1969. After all, many management techniques such as forecasting, operations research and financial control require relatively few staff to operate. The probability which awaits future testing on more detailed employment breakdowns is that most of the staff increases in companies such as Dunlop have been mainly administrative in character.

There is finally a consideration which may go some way towards accounting for the reluctance of organisations to reduce indirect staffs when their levels of activity and/or performance turn down. The recruitment of suitably qualified staff personnel may be difficult, time consuming and costly. In some cases the full benefit of applying their expertise to the particular circumstances and problems of the organisation may take months, even years, in realisation. It would therefore be unwise to treat such employees as variable costs, whereas (subject to the ethics and costs of redundancy) the ease of firing and re-hiring semiskilled and unskilled operatives is significantly greater. In Britain, moreover, where the public sector competes quite success-fully with the private sector in attracting better qualified employees, it could be a wise policy to provide some staff with job security even if in the short run it cannot be justified economically.

This last argument perhaps helps to explain the infrequency with which the number of indirects contracts in periods of decline or difficulty, but it cannot explain why it then tends to rise during periods of operative re-recruitment. Indeed, none of the explanations advanced in this section can account wholly satisfactorily for the employment trends found in Dunlop and reported for the American organisations. The suspicion remains that the inflation of the indirect component in part reflects problems of management control and organisation.

Implications for management

More evidence needs to be collected before one can draw the firm
conclusion that a non-productive component is proliferating within the
British productive sector. Data are required from other major companies to see whether their experience is similar to Dunlop's. It would
also be desirable to break staff employment down into its constituent
components so as to distinguish more precisely between administrative,
clerical and technical categories of indirect staff. Technical and
specialist staff might perhaps be considered as less of a pure 'overhead'.
Assuming, in the meantime, that the problem is a general and serious
one, it has to be regarded in part as a weakness in the managerial
control of resources. How is this to be analysed? What are its likely
consequences if left uncontrolled? Are there some policies which may
reduce the problem?

The cynic might conclude that it is simply a case of the staff man
exercising his influence over employment policy so as to feather his own
nest. This is essentially Parkinson's reasoning. There may be some
truth in this explanation, but the problem also has to be analysed at the
more general level of management organisation. What seems to have
been taking place is a process of increasing organisational complexity
over time. Complexity can be assessed in the first instance in terms of
the numbers of different job and departmental specialisms which are
found in a firm or other kind of institution. Encouragement to pro-
liferate specialisms is provided both by growth which appears to offer
opportunities for additional division of labour as an economy of scale
and by the development of new techniques, some valuable and some
merely faddish, which appeal to management as new essentials to take
on board. Specialist positions and functions multiply, and so do staff
numbers accordingly.

Increases in complexity add to difficulties of control and co-ordination. Lawrence and Lorsch have indicated that the higher the internal
differentiation of an organisation, the more problematic it is to
maintain its integration at an adequate level. The traditional response
to problems of control and co-ordination has been to institute more
job and task definitions, more procedures, more formal meetings and
other marks of bureaucratic formalisation. This generates extra paperwork. Additional administrative and support staff are required to devise
the new systems and to service them. They may understandably come
to feel that their continued employment is best assured by maintaining
the steady advance of formalisation. The growth of indirect staff in

turn tends to raise organisational complexity and so elements of a self-reinforcing vicious spiral begins to emerge. Studies of business and other types of organisation have generally confirmed that there is in practice a close association between their level of internal complexity and of formalisation (Child, 1973a). Another facet of this process is that, due to necessary limitations in managerial spans of control, the number of management levels tends to be inflated as indirects increase. This generates further communication problems up and down the hierarchy, encouraging in turn the institution of new vertical information systems and additional staff to run these. So it is quite possible for significant increases in the non-productive component of a company to be generated not so much as a function of personal empire building, but as part of an organisational process which can get out of control. There is in addition a well-known tendency of organisations to become more bureaucratic as they grow older, through the attempts to encapsulate their learning experience into standardised problem-solving procedures. That, too, tends to add to the administrative staff component which services such procedures.

The proliferation of staff employees is non-productive to the extent that the processes just described are avoidable. Indeed, it can be extremely costly. First, additional staff overheads mount up. Second, insofar as a company becomes more complex with growing specialisation and staff members, the net result for direct personnel and their line managers may well be to consume more of their time in communication, discussion and conflict resolution than would otherwise be the case; this is despite the ostensible purpose of having staff to relieve the line's burden. Third, the proliferation of staff employees is likely to make any effective participation of direct employees in decision making more difficult to achieve by injecting the mystique of the so-called expert which calls for special prerogatives in decision making, and by contributing to an extension of management hierarchies which can only serve to increase perceived distance and genuine ignorance of each other between the top and bottom of organisations. In the long term, thwarted participation and increased distance within our productive organisations may prove to be the most costly concomitant of a growing non-productive component.

It is particularly important to take the matter further and to make an assessment of the full extent of the problem, because the means do exist to exercise more control over increases in the non-productive component and in the bureaucratic mode of administration which tends to accompany them. These methods are described elsewhere at some length (Child, 1977), and are now merely summarised.

First, the number of different specialists has to be kept to a minimum. This may mean securing services and information from outside the organisation as and when necessary rather than maintaining an internal staff overhead. It may also mean exploring the possibilities for enlarging the scope of specialist jobs so that a smaller number can cope with a given range of activities. Carefully designed, this could provide a basis for job enrichment and personal development for specialist staff. In some organisations, duplication of staff functions could be avoided by amalgamating these into central units; this is one of the rationales for the current reorganisation of British Airways. There may even be areas where an activity hived off into a specialised function could be reincorporated back into line management, or even delegated to the operative level. Indeed, experiments in job enrichment and the formation of autonomous working groups have usually involved the incorporation of some indirect activities such as inspection, work planning and routine maintenance into direct work.

Second, administration has to be simplified as a prerequisite for reducing the numbers of administrators. This speaks for more use to be made of direct contact between members of different departments as a basis for co-ordination instead of relying upon co-ordination via formal procedures, elaborate plans or formal meetings with a paraphernalia of papers and minutes which have to be serviced by administrative staff. Simple action lists are required rather than complex minutes which moulder in files, only recalled to support a political point. Trust and mutual understanding are superior bases for working together than any formal arrangement. Management by objectives, as it is intended to work, eliminates time and effort aimed at regulating how people carry out their work and instead directs attention to the evaluation of a few key results. All these features are among the components of a management philosophy aimed at simplifying administration, and reducing the number of administrators. They cannot be introduced overnight into a situation in which people's experience of management leaves them expecting to be heavily administered, but they point to a way out of the problem of proliferating non-productive activity.

Sheane, a consultant working in ICI, has been particularly forthright on the need to reduce the burden of bureaucracy in a discussion paper on *Why do managers join unions?* Sheane argues that a bureaucratic style of administration makes managers feel that they have little opportunity to develop through assuming responsibility, that they are invisible and subject only to efficiency assessments. This leads to a displacement of individual communication by collective bargaining, through a process of managerial unionisation. This then reduces the

tolerance and goodwill shown towards the company, and in turn
reduces the company's ability to introduce changes necessary to its
long term survival. Among the solutions which Sheane advocates are
for managers at all levels themselves to question 'the various forms of
bureaucracy used in the name of "control", "improvement", "holding
the system together", or whatever plausible public banner under which
it is presented'. More senior positions should be on a short contract
basis in order to reduce administrative entrenchment. Formal and
bureaucratic processes should be gradually transformed into informal
ones, and new systems or bureaucratic procedures rejected however
plausible. In this way, formal committees should become transformed
into 'working' meetings on real issues; formal written one-way
communications should become two-way communication sessions
with dialogue; sitting in one's office relying on the 'formal system' to
find out what has happened should become transformed into getting
out and visiting people in their place of work, relying on a direct
informal network to discover what is going on and what will happen.
All this should help to cut back the numbers of administrators,
secretaries and office personnel required, and at the same time improve
the quality of management.

Third and finally, moves towards despecialisation and simplified
administration are likely to be facilitated by the devolution of autonomy
to smaller business units. This, is the principle of management by
objectives applied to whole business units within a firm. If certain
support functions must for reasons of economy or policy preserve a
specialised identity, these can remain centralised, as already
mentioned. In other respects, the use of smaller operating units with
low internal complexity should help to reduce the proportion of non-
productive employment. Other advantages associated with this policy
may well include the higher level of general morale which is normally
associated with smaller units, and the possibility that the small or
medium size unit matches more precisely the bounds of a given
business area. The divisions of many companies have today grown too
large and diversified for their activity to be focused on a single market
and/or technology, and this too speaks in favour of further devolution
in order to reduce their complexity.

Summary

The problem of non-productive activity is not confined, as Bacon and Eltis imply, to the non-market sector of the economy. It is also present within the so-called productive sector, including manufacturing. Judging by the evidence so far available, the indirect component within the productive sector is growing more than proportionately. The general argument advanced by Bacon and Eltis implies that any growth in non-productive employment should be brought under greater management control within enterprises. It has been possible to outline some practical lines of action to that end. However, further more detailed research is required to help managers judge who are the non-productive people within the indirect component. This would entail detailed breakdowns of indirect employment and comparisons between companies taking into account their type of activity, scale of operation, level of performance, mode of organisation and other relevant factors.

Appendix 1
Administrative proliferation in the British Admiralty 1914–1967

	1914	1928	1938	1948	1958	1964	1967
Total number of vessels in commission	542	317	308	413	238	182	114
Officers and men in Royal Navy	125000	90700	89500	134400	94900	84900	83900
Dockyard workers	57000	62439	39022	48252	40164	41563	37798
Dockyard officials and clerical staff	3249	4558	4423	6120	6219	7395	8013
Admiralty officials and clerical staff	4366	7729	11270	31636	32237	32035	33574

Source: C Northcote Parkinson, *The Law of Delay,* John Murray, London, 1970, p 4.

References

Bacon R and Eltis W, *Britain's Economic Problem: Too few Producers,* Macmillan, 1976
—'Too few producers: the drift Healey must stop', *Sunday Times,* 14 November 1976
Child J, 'Predicting and understanding organisation structure', *Administrative Science Quarterly,* Vol 18, 1973(a)
—'Parkinson's progress: accounting for the number of specialists in organisations', *Administrative Science Quarterly,* Vol 18, 1973(b)
—*Organisation: A Guide to Problems and Practice,* Harper and Row, 1977
Freeman J H and Hannan M T, 'Growth and decline processes in organisations' *American Sociological Review,* Vol 40, 1975
Hendershot G E and James T F, 'Size and growth as determinants of administrative–production ratios in organisations', *American Sociological Review,* Vol 37, 1972
Lawrence P R and Lorsch J W, *Organisation and Environment,* Boston: Division of Research, Graduate School of Business Administration, Harvard University, 1967
Parkinson C N, *Parkinson's Law or the Pursuit of Progress,* John Murray, 1958
—*The Law of Delay,* John Murray, 1970
Sheane D, 'Why do managers join unions?', unpublished paper, 1975
Tsouderos J E, 'Organisational change in terms of a series of selective variables', *American Sociological Review,* Vol 20, 1955

Authority and task in manufacturing operations of multinational firms

Alistair Mant

The author is an independent consultant. This paper
was written as a report on work done for the
Department of Industry

Introduction

This is a report on a small-scale study which had two precedents:
(a) The fact that British manufacturing operations appear to be less productive than their Continental counterparts.
(b) That the multinational firm, especially the foreign-based one, is likely to be a fruitful source of explanation about these differences.

The study therefore had two main elements:
(c) A review of comparative productivity data in order to ascertain if (a) above is correct.
(d) A programme of interviews with senior executives in multinational firms, especially those executives situated on organisational boundaries between countries.

The study was a small-scale one, essentially exploratory in nature and ought not to be seen as anything more; however, the issues are undoubtedly important.

Approach

The main interviews were conducted with senior executives and key line managers and staff in eleven companies. Interviews were also conducted with academics who have made a special study of productivity and management development policies and practices in the multinational firm. Also, we looked tentatively into patterns of employment in a group of new towns in order to ascertain, if we could, whether the FBMNS were now in a position to attract a particular, entrepreneurial element in the work force. The selection of the firms themselves was somewhat eclectic, bearing in mind the exploratory nature of the study. One firm, for example, was included because we discovered that they had recently had to release their German General Manager in Germany, and replace him with an Englishman; another because it has unrivalled knowledge about comparable international productivity; one of the Swedish firms because we felt that Swedes working under British mangement in a British factory might provide us with some insight into differing assumptions; others because they were outstandingly successful in particular British manufacturing sites and notably 'Swedish' in their approach; another because our hypothesis about the capacity to fight constructively (in role) appeared to resonate closely with their experience in establishing a factory in Britain.

The focus throughout has been principally on manufacturing operations, not because we were unmindful of weaknesses elsewhere, but because it is here that productivity differentials are so inexplicably wide in relation to foreign competition.

Productivity

All the data suggest that British manufacturing in Britain is, on average, less productive than the vast majority of manufacturing operations elsewhere. The pattern in the few foreign-based multinationals (FBMN) we saw is for productivity in their British subsidiaries to be lower than at home, but still higher than in comparable British operations. Many of the FBMNS are puzzled about the scale of the differences, given that the 'tempo of work' in Britain appears to be similar to that in comparable, say, Swedish factories. The FBMN conclusion is that crucial differences must occur in management.

This view is reinforced by some of the comparative studies. Pratten, for example, found productivity differentials of 50 per cent between North American and United Kingdom firms and differentials of 27 per cent and 15 per cent respectively with Germany and France. He attempted to distinguish whether these differentials were primarily accounted for by economic or behavioural factors. As to the Continental operations he took 'behavioural' factors, especially 'manning and efficiency', to be as important in accounting for the differentials as 'economic' ones. Only in the USA did he regard the size of the market and the length of production run as the prime factor. Notably, differentials in the age of plant and machinery and the incidence of strikes and restrictive practices were not thought to be of paramount importance. Instead, and especially in the Anglo–German comparison, United Kingdon managerial performance and quality, poor systems of production control, lack of attention to methods of production and capital utilisation, slack management controls leading to excessive waiting time, ineffective manning levels, and so on, were cited most often. There appears, in other words, to be a differential commitment and attention to detail in the immediate supporting (management) systems of production, as between British junior management and their overseas counterparts.

On the basis of this study, and the available evidence, we postulate a network of productivity differentials something like this:

	In UK		Overseas	
Indigenous firms	1	Low	2	High
UK multinationals	3	Medium	4	High
Foreign multinationals	5	High	6	High*

* Box 6 ought perhaps to read very high, relative to boxes 5 and 2 in particular

We have insufficient evidence about the performance of the overseas manufacturing operations of British multinational firms. What we do have suggests that they are broadly comparable with competing foreign firms; this implies that, given the 'tempo of work' argument, the crucial factor is to have non-British foremen, supervisors, first-line managers, etc, in the supporting system. Cross-cultural productivity comparisons are notoriously difficult to make due to complexity, except in certain single-product industries such as motors and ship-building, where one can compute the quantities of direct and indirect labour required to produce one ship or one car, or whatever; but the matrix represents the best assessment of available facts.

Swedish views on British manufacturing

We began the study by talking to a very senior group of managers, all of them with experience of British manufacturing sites and currently in the head offices of Swedish MNCs, for their views of British manufacturing. Some of the themes are summarised below:

(1) *'Management' versus work*   The British manager's self-concept is of *being* a 'manager' rather than *doing* a particular kind of work with particular, valued outputs.

(2) *Ambition*   In that context, the British manager is found to be more overtly ambitious for higher management rank; the Swede more modest in the expression of aspirations.

(3) *Creativity*   British machine development proposals consistently have a speculative 'blue sky' character, *vis-à-vis* all other countries, though the ideas are frequently very creative.

(4) *Detail*   By contrast, British manufacturing managers are seen to

abhor detail and to assume, usually incorrectly, that attention to detail may be readily delegated downwards. For example: 'Why don't they keep the factory clean? – it must be connected with productivity!'

(5) *Involvement with work*   Further, British manufacturing managers are felt to lack fundamental interest in the technologies they have to manage; they have not the 'hobby' status as with some of their foreign counterparts.

(6) *Human relations and work*   Human relations in British subsidiaries is seen therefore to contain an essential 'phoneyness' because of dissociation from the work in the foreground; the technology and the throughput.

(7) *Relationships versus work*   The pride of the British managers, production and otherwise, is felt to be in 'profit and relationships' rather than the throughput.

(8) *Sales versus manufacturing*   Accordingly, in some cases, the British sales operation was seen as outstanding within European operations. For all the firms, the verdict on British manufacturing operations could be summarised as only 'fair, could do better'.

These observations are important in the light of the thrust of the productivity comparisons noted above, especially those which point to slackness in the controls exercised by lower levels of British manufacturing management as being the crucial issue. What these observations suggest is that British manufacturing managers, once they achieve 'managerial' rank tend more than their Continental counterparts, to regard themselves as having undergone a change of kind rather than degree. They are, so to speak, no longer in manufacturing, but in management. The very existence of the extensive English-language 'management movement' largely unparalleled on the Continent supports, as Fores and Glover have argued, the idea of a separate, split-off 'generalist' management role, somewhat detached from work itself.

The comparatively low status of British industry as a whole and of manufacturing management and rewards in particular, reflects the apparent need for forms of role legitimation, apart from the process of manufacturing itself. In sociological language, the British manufacturing manager is 'committed' to his role, in the sense of coercion through impersonally-enforced arrangements, but not 'attached' to it (personal choice and self-image). These are not new observations; but for realistic research to be pursued in relation to them, there is a need for some theoretical framework which will provide explanations, and help to make predictions about the outcomes of possible initiatives. This paper adopts an authority framework because the evidence suggests that 'management' status in Britain is commonly associated with the elevation of status, *per se*; so it is dissociated from the intrinsic authority of task systems themselves.

The distinction between inter-personal and inter-role relationships

Figure 5.1 illustrates the difference between relationships between individuals and those between roles in the context of a shared task.

The former model may be characteristic of a relationship based solely on personal power, the latter as based on authority, deriving from roles in relation to a task. A simple illustration is the difference between two people who choose to live together for as long as it suits them, and another two who decide jointly to enter into the institution of marriage and to take up appropriate roles in relation to the institution. The one is essentially dyadic, the other triangualar. This is not to suggest that personal power may not be deployed in role, rather the

Figure 5.1

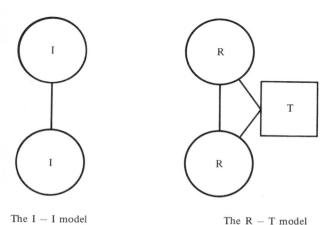

The I − I model   The R − T model

reverse: that an authoritative role provides a sound base for the mobilisation of whatever personal power the individual may happen to have.

Extrinsic and intrinsic tasks

Plainly the R–T model reflects the formal authority of an organisation, the agreed basis on which work is done. In systems theory, the dominant conversion process of a manufacturing system is the conversion of raw materials, components, etc, into a finished product of requisite quality to generate adequate revenue, after costs, to purchase further raw materials, knowledge, people, capital equipment, etc, in order to sustain the system: to survive. A manufacturing sub-system of a firm has many throughputs; but the product is the dominant one from which, ultimately, all authority is derived. This may be said to be the normal Swedish assumption: irrespective of hierarchical level, the manufacturing task serves as the basis of role relationships, and especially the role relationship between worker and foreman/supervisor/first-line manager.

By contrast, Swedish descriptions of British manufacturing management suggest, at worst, a network of straightforward power relationships, or, possibly, an ambiguous role relationship within which the manager attempts to derive his 'authority' from sources extrinsic to the task: that is, from 'management' status. The extrinsic management task suggested by the Swedish observations of Britain is that of 'getting ahead'; it is almost as if the provision of managerial career opportunities was the dominant task of the British system, and manufacturing simply a constraint upon that.

This is, perhaps, to put the case too baldly. All organisations represent the conjunction of task systems and human aspirations. The balance of these different interests is, however, crucial. The postulated Swedish balance would seem, at the very least, to be a logical one, something which may not be lost on British workers operating under foreign management assumptions. As Nichols has observed of chemical workers, workers may be more concerned with the *competence* of their management (to pursue the intrinsic task), than the extent to which they pursue 'human relations', 'industrial democracy' and other, doubtless worthwhile, pursuits extrinsic to the central task. Our enquiries in the new towns strongly reinforced this idea.

Seen thus, the current emphasis on human relations in industry may be misconceived, unless it is set in the context of task, role and

Figure 5.2

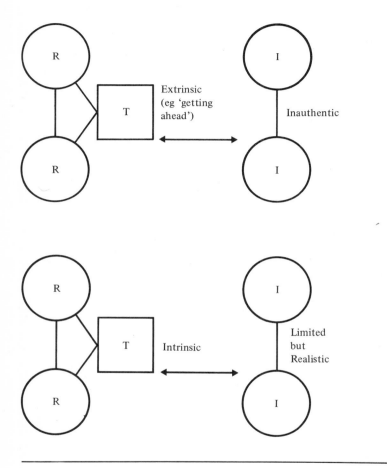

authority. Good human relations does not ensure good management. However, good management cannot occur except in a setting of appropriate (role) relationships between people. Another way of expressing this is to say that an extrinsic task-assumption will lead to inauthentic interpersonal relationships ('phoney', as the Swedes put it); an intrinsic assumption will lead to limited, but authentic, ones.

Industrial relations implications of the extrinsic assumption

The hypothesised splitting of British first-line management from the manufacturing task-system may be associated with two familiar phenomena of 'industrial relations':

(a) If workers find themselves without leadership in relation to the intrinsic task, it is not illogical for them to seek it elsewhere, on the assumption that everyone requires leadership to some extent. The leadership vacuum is commonly filled by the shop steward, a person who, unlike many members of first-line management, at least appears to be clear in his mind about what he is fighting for. See section on 'Fight' below.

(b) We ought not to be surprised by the prevalence of restrictive practices around workers' demarcation lines, when the pursuit of extrinsic tasks or of 'management' status by managers represents a form of demarcation line between 'management' and work itself. Clearly, the destructive elements in the attitudes of both management and workers in Britain are mutually supporting. It is not, however, commonly recognised the extent to which worker assumptions represent a mirror-image of their bosses' assumptions.

Task structures and the capacity to fight

An important outcome of the 'intrinsic' assumption noted above is that it provides an agreed, safe structure within which conflict can be confronted and coped with. To quote Rice: 'The problem in industry is not fight itself, but the assurance that the fights will occur between the right people, about the right issues, at the right time.' In a power relationship, or an ambiguous role relationship, Fight is always a threatening thing and its outcomes are frequently destructive. But to fight about important task issues, from within an agreed role, allows the possibility of stepping out of that role into another one with 'no hard feelings'. Clearly, British manufacturing industry is not without fight, but there is abundant evidence that the fighting is often displaced from task-related issues. British 'industrial relations' activity is, to put it bluntly, usually more politicised than elsewhere.

I raise the issue of fight here because, in the course of this study, certain curious similarities began to emerge in the histories of the FBMNs we studied. In almost every case there was a celebrated fight in the company folklore; in each case it was a fight with the superordinate overseas system about a task-related issue. Because, in each case the fight was remembered, it appeared to serve as a kind of informal bench-mark – the sticking point for conflict with higher authority. In one case, unsatisfactory profitability was dealt with by the quick deployment of external consultants; in another, slipping production standards, by the sending in of head office 'trainers'. In each of these cases, the superordinate FBMN system defined the presenting problem as a technical one, rather than an 'industrial relations' one.

This provides us with some evidence that the overriding model in the minds of the non-British superior managers was of authority derived from the task system, rather than simply from rank. Neither were they afraid to fight about important issues, because they believe themselves to be so authorised. More correctly, they would be prepared to fight (on technical grounds) but seldom have to do so in reality because the underlying logic of their approach appears to have led, in each case, to harmonious industrial/task relations. To quote one of the Swedish manufacturing managers: 'With the British we find it is all right when they have got it that they have to do it!' Moreover, it seems that these fights had historical/symbolic importance. It was as though they represented a threshold beyond which the system had to pass into a mature working relationship, just as children have to determine the sticking point of their parents, their teachers, and so on, in order to establish a workable boundary for their own independence.

A much publicised case, which we were able to look at briefly, is that of a Japanese electronics firm which elected to fight, in the end successfully, over the wearing of overalls by all staff, management included. This is a particularly interesting case because it so clearly represents the importation of alien social ideas to a British manufacturing site. Furthermore, it is an idea from a country which outperforms all others in the productivity leagues. The same firm is markedly more productive than comparable American firms, even in America. Most significantly, the uniform/overall symbolises the shared task: whatever your seniority, your ultimate authority derives from the manufactured products going out the factory door. As in the other cases mentioned, this British factory appears to be settling down to its task-orientation, and its overalls, as if nothing could be more natural. The essential logic of it does not escape British workers, management or otherwise. Additionally, the military model of organisation is not yet dead in British industrial culture, although it is presently much discredited. Some aspects of it, such as old fashioned attitudes to the primacy of task-authority and close attention to detail, appear to be more important for success than unsupported creativity.

This Japanese company's decision-making process in establishing a British factory is significant. The key elements were:
(a) The selection of a locally-born factory manager with 'participative' experience in manufacturing management. In fact, the firm's Japanese United Kingdom Director is a devotee of socio-technical systems thinking; and the factory manager was carefully chosen from the well-known Glacier–Tavistock network.
(b) A close study of FBMN and British factories with a successful track record in manufacturing. The conclusion was that there was nothing at all wrong with British workers, given good management. As the factory manager now says of his one-time itinerant TV-repairmen: 'We had to get them mentally attuned to our standards and flexibility.'
    It would be wrong to overgeneralise about this particular site. Very few members of the management team are over 40, and the predominantly female work-force is drawn from an area of relatively high unemployment. Nonetheless, the aspects in common with Swedish management are striking even though Swedish manufacturing represents a distinctly different culture from Japanese:
(a) An unfailing concentration on the output of the task system by all parties. The Convener of shop stewards regards his district office as a place to go only in case of 'failure': 'I like to keep them out as much as possible'.
(b) An 'almost pedantic' approach to standards: 'You must get it right the first time, which takes time; and if the set has a tiny scratch on it, it won't go out'. Interestingly, the Japanese will not tolerate cumulative target graphs on the factory wall; it is surmised because they divert workers' attention from quality to speed and the possibility of 'pacing'.
(c) The capacity to fight, in role:reference the overalls.

Fight and dependence   To be technical, the issues here are those of psychological Dependence. Elsewhere (Mant, 1977) I have employed the family analogy to suggest that a family unit capable (probably through its breadwinner) of fighting successfully in the environment for its survival, may well have a Dependent structure within. That internal dependence would be a mature dependence if the right people really were able to fight with the right people about the right issues. I contrasted two sorts of families, which are familiar to most social workers:

Family A
(1) Firm but flexible assumptions about standards of behaviour and performance.
(2) High time involvement with the children.
(3) Carefully regulated, low-key money allowances.
(4) Secure financial base.
(5) Mature dependency assumptions
(6) Tested and elaborated authority of family roles related to family norms.

Family B
(1) Double standards of behaviour and performance.
(2) Low and grudging time involvement with the children.
(3) Emphasis on spasmodic and lavish gifts and pocket money.
(4) Insecure financial base.
(5) Immature dependency or Fight/Flight assumptions.
(6) Power structure.

Unhappily, the 'problem family' B will do as an archetype for the problem firm in Britain. It is a place where the rhetoric of money has taken over from more intrinsic, work-related matters. However, it is well known that children from background B are able to adapt fairly readily to the A setting, though not without a fight and not without certain residual identity problems. The British, as we can see, are able to work for foreigners and appear to respond well to their methods.

Absent leadership   The success of the FBMNs in Britain may, as these accounts suggest, be simply a product of the underlying, and communicable, logic of the task-oriented approach. That is, that if authority derives from task, in the long run, it will not be confused with 'authoritarianism', which I take to be the use, or abuse, of mere positional power. In fact, the FBMNs we looked at are very diverse. As one researcher put it, of three Japanese firms operating in this country: 'One is just like a Japanese company, another just like an American one, and the third seems to everyone there to be English'.

However, since the Second World War Britain has, to a significant extent, as I have argued elsewhere (Mant, 1977), assumed that leadership in the taking of painful industrial decisions must come from elsewhere, notably America. Historically, this had little to do with logic, with the rightness of American methods for British culture, and much to do with a profound disillusionment with the capacity of British mangers to cope with the fights that emerge when change is implemented. We have therefore to consider whether the assumption of Absent Leadership is now so deep that it has an independent existence: that is, that irrespective of the underlying logic of management methods, foreigners are automatically assumed by certain types of British employee to be better employers and better managers than British ones. It is plausible that foreigners may be untainted by the negative class projections directed towards British top management. In this reading, the FBMNs may have the capacity to attract some of the ablest and most ambitious people, almost irrespective of the firm's quality, with a consequent long-term impact on productivity.

Success stories

It would be wrong to leave a discussion on Absent Leadership without commenting on examples of British success in comparable multi-national firms. In the course of the study, we looked at two such examples of successful manufacturing operations in Britain, one within a British multinational and the other in a foreign-based one. The FBMN subsidiary is part of a world-wide network of 'product-by-plant' manufacturing sites and thus its performance in Britain is fairly readily compared with that of other sites within the firm. The British multinational operation is, in fact, the main plant of a subsidiary company of a major group. Thus, it has a distinctive identity within the group and comparisons must therefore be drawn from competition. If we accept the logic put forward by the Swedish managers, then our hypothesis would be that when British manufacturing operations are spectacularly successful, as in these two cases, we would expect to find a top management closely involved with details down the line as well as attending to the generalities. Further, one would expect to find close identification of workers with their management, based on joint identification with the task system: to quote one Swede: 'Why don't the British educate people *not* born in flower beds?'.

Let me deal, as a case-study, with the British company site. It is a medium-sized (3–5000) manufacturing operation, with a long tradition on the site, exporting a high proportion of its output. The firm is rated a 'superior vendor' by the main US firms it supplies; a source of great pride to them and a considerable tribute to their sustained capacity to deliver on time and to specification. Its manufacturing manager was suggested to me as a suitable subject, as a result of a discussion with the collected top managers of the group. Essentially my question was: 'What is your most successful manufacturing operation, and who are the people most responsible for that?' One member of my audience mentioned that the manufacturing manager in question gave him the

best advice of his career, namely 'The best part of the day is between
7.15 and 8.15 am on the factory floor!' It seemed appropriate to arrange
an extended interview with this man.

In practice, he was as predicted:

(a) His repute is 'rough but fair' (his words). He clearly works at least
as hard and long as anyone on the site.

(b) Mutual identification is high. 'I've got the best shop committee in
the business; and they can tell me to get stuffed!'

(c) Conflict is possible and direct and relevant (see above).

(d) Boundary maintenance is firm but flexible and the dependence in
the system adequate for its needs. For example, managers whose
career horizons are limited are often 'fixed up' outside the company
and all promotions come from within. Also: 'We are never stuck for
components'.

(e) Pride in standards is high: 'You can't buy my buyers': 'If I say I'll
deliver on a certain date, then I will'.

The man himself comes from working class origins, is proud of his
achievements and takes great and uncomplicated pride in his company
Jaguar and the other appurtenances of office. He knows almost everyone on the site by name and uses written communications as infrequently as possible, in the interests of speed.

He is, in fact, not an unfamiliar figure in British manufacturing
industry – a focal, Brunel-like entrepreneurial figure, ruthlessly
dedicated to task performance. The puzzle is to know whether to regard
the surrounding system as predominantly an authority structure, R–T,
or a power network, I–I. At an obvious level, it is a highly successful
task system, uncompromising in delivering the goods on time at the
right quality. Yet the manufacturing manager is a more flamboyant,
charismatic figure than one would expect to find in a Swedish factory.
He is aware of this, of the massive psychological projections he has to
absorb: 'Everyone's watching you!' He swears a great deal, almost as
if he is required to in order to maintain his identification with the
workers. He is also, despite his high intelligence, anti-intellectual.

The charisma is clearly important, as though British workers are too
wedded to the notion of the charismatic leader and not well-adapted to
limited leadership roles in a shared-task context: as J K Galbraith has
commented, of politics: 'The Swiss simply solve problems; the British
search for a leader to solve them'. Equally important may be this man's
construction of his management approach. He refers, with conviction,
to 'the vehicle' – a kind of shared model of the main factory processes
which, although abstract, can be grasped down the line by everyone
who matters. Most important to him, it (the vehicle) has 'not had the

soul taken out of the job' by computer print-outs. In describing the 'vehicle' this man is, in fact, putting forward an almost perfect exposition of the R–T conception of authority; role relationships regulated by shared commitment to a task conception.

As I noted before this is a highly successful operation, yet one has to note that the burden of the charismatic model on the top manager is very considerable. He will, at the very least, be difficult to replace, always a good test of the existence of a task system versus a power network. In Britain, the scarcity in high places of those 'not born in flower-beds', and who have not lost contact with detail, probably makes it inevitable that those who do win through are saddled with a disproportionately heavy burden of personal leadership. A Swedish senior manager, say, would have much in common with this man, but be less burdened with the dependent projections of others. The system described is technically a mature dependent one, but with much of the Fight carried by one man. It is highly effective, but essentially unstable.

The other anecdote cannot be described in full here. I note it briefly for contrast, because the other manufacturing manager, with responsibility for two manufacturing sites and a distribution depot operates rather from the Fight Basic Assumption, as opposed to the Dependent one. In other respects these two men are similar as to background, attitude to the management job (attention to detail, close involvement, etc), repute and success. In this case, however, the manager has a running battle with his warehousemen and their union, and they with him. This is a ritualised, internal fight, once again, not uncommon in British factories. It is a largely pointless fight but, given the other virtues of the system, its effects appear to be marginal. The first manager, it should be noted, has 'communists' in bogey status, but believes he is able to 'keep them out' through an laborate screening process. Both of these managers' approaches might be thought somewhat quirky by a Swede: the one dominatingly paternal, the other more avuncular; but the point is that their operations run like well-oiled machines. What these operations have in common, apart from their success, is their bosses' natural affinity with the assumptive base of the Swedish top managers.

Here, I have dealt over-briefly with two very complex circumstances. The implications are that we ought to devote much more research attention to *successful* prime movers both in manufacturing and top management. We do not properly understand why it works when it does, although I hope this throws some light on the subject; and we do not understand the ways in which organisational systems cluster round the successful men. There are implications here also for the further study of the boundary between school/university and manufacturing industry and the nature of the guidance provided to prospective entrants. Most young people want to enter the 'professions', whatever that means nowadays: see also Glover's first paper in this book. The R–T model is, in fact, a re-statement of the professional position, the establishment of a workable, limited role-relationship in the context of shared assumptions about task (the 'vehicle'). Doubtless, most young graduates see industry as a world of power, on the I–I model. How careers advisers and appointments officers see it, is difficult to say.

There is, however, abundant evidence that, as the school system has become increasingly politicised in recent years, in much the same way as many firms; so it has become harder for pupils, and staff, to identify the intrinsic R–T elements of their own systems. When children left school at 14, the transition to work symbolised the beginning of adulthood and the assumed necessity to Fight in the real world. One result of the raised school-leaving age has been the export of young adults to the world of work many of whom now leave school in a state of what has been described as 'resourceless dependence' because nothing in their experience of the role of Pupil has helped them to grasp the R–T model. The outcome is an incapacity to mobilise con-constructuve Fight. Thus, they are frightened of industry, unmindful of its realistic authority and entirely ill-equipped to see conflict as part of life, manageable in-role.

Conclusion

Perhaps the most important conclusion to come from this work is that many people know it already. When foreign firms simply behave logically they do not introduce new ideas to Britain but remind us of something we have previously taken for granted in other kinds of institutions: in, for example, the family, the school, the church and so on. An aspect of the 'absent leadership' phenomenon since the war, has been the largely uncritical adoption of new (usually American), complex 'management techniques'. Many have been necessary, and useful, but the process has tended to submerge some of the simplicities which still persist in the best British firms and, as I argue here, in many FBMNS. Those simplicities may well inform the lives of British workers and their managers when they are not at work; working for a FBMN may simply provide a way of taking one's values and standards to work with one instead of having to leave them at home.

If this makes sense, the educational task in British industry has not to do with the acquisition of new knowledge, but the liberation of old wisdom. Not all of the educators can be expected to measure up to, or even understand, that task.

References

Principal references on productivity
Central Policy Review Staff, *Report on the Future of the British Car Industry*, HMSO, 1975
Dunning H, 'United States industry in Britain', *Financial Times*, 1974
Huston T and Dunning J H, 'United Kingdom industry abroad', *Financial Times*, 1976
Panić M (ed), *The United Kingdom and West German Manufacturing Industry 1954–1972: A Comparison of Structure and Performance*, NEDO, 1976
Pratten C F, *A Comparison of The Performance of Swedish and United Kingdom Companies*, Cambridge University Press, 1976
—*Labour Productivity Differentials Within International Companies*, Cambridge University Press, 1976
United States Senate Committee on Finance (Chairman Russell B Long), *Implications of multinational Firms for World Trade and Labour*, US Government Printing Office, Washington, 1973

Other references
Department of Education and Science, *Ten Good Schools*, HMSO, 1977
Fores M and Glover I, 'The real work of executives', *Management Today*, November 1976
Hudson L, 'Making things: a psychologist's view', Paper Seven in this book
Mant A D, *The Rise and Fall of the British Manager*, Macmillan, 1977
—*An Open Systems Model of Business School Activity*, SSRC research report, October 1975
—*et al, Towards Managerial Development for Tomorrow*, TSA research report, September 1975
Miller E J and Rice A K, *Systems of Organisation*, Tavistock, 1967
Nichols T and Beynon H, *Living with Capitalism: Case Relations and the Modern Factory*, Routledge, 1977
Reed B D and Bazalgette J, 'Education for mature responsibility', unpublished paper submitted to Secretary of State for Education, February 1977

The management tradition: a continental view

Arndt Sorge
INTERNATIONAL INSTITUTE OF MANAGEMENT, BERLIN

When this paper was written the author was a research
fellow at St Antony's College, Oxford

Management tradition or management fad?

It must signify a high degree of social acceptance of management as an idea, a movement and a profession, that there should be a session of this conference under the title of 'the management tradition'. At least that acceptance is valid for Britain. In Germany, there has been since the war a wave of new ideas about management to the extent that the word itself has become incorporated into the German language. But it is highly doubtful whether one can speak of a 'management tradition' in that country. In particular, the Anglo-Saxon idea of management as a unified profession did not catch on in the same way as it did in Britain.

So what are the connotations of the German word 'Manager'? It denotes above all a specific outlook of a manager, in the English sense, towards his job. He would profess a liking for '*modernes Management*', which has become a set phrase; this means that he sees himself as a dynamic, unconventional businessman without any patriarchal allure, driving his subordinates hard, but taking care to 'motivate' them and give them satisfying work to do; he usually wears American-style clothes, sometimes taking off his coat and rolling up his shirt-sleeves. His eyes are keenly fixed on profits and growth, he has matter-of-fact ways which however do not preclude outbreaks of folksy humour. Although loyal to his firm, he personally does not care whether he manages oil, dish-washers, oranges and lemons, or mortgages. Then we get to the rather more negative connotations to the German mind: he has no intrinsic attachment to what happens to be his 'throughput'. This is why he is regarded as a jack-of-all-trades, dabbling in all kinds of things here and there, without serious dedication to a well-defined life-time activity. He has a rather blurred identity, in view of the traditional images of the identity of *Techniker, Kaufmann* (commercial man), and their ramifications.

This negative connotation was strongest shortly after the term itself was introduced into the German language; then it hardly referred to managers in industry, but primarily to people who organised boxing matches, or ran a circus or a road show. The 'Manager', thus, at first was a label for a certain astuteness in emptying the common man's pockets by just putting on a show without being able to perform in it, for a roving occupation bordering on vagrancy. Heinz Hartmann has given a vivid account of the early history of the term in the German language, and he shows how that label got stuck to a certain extent, so that a 'Manager' is partly suspect to this day. It was hard to find an equivalent to the English term in the German language, as the predominant ideology made a sharp difference between *Führung* and

Leitung, the former being the entrepreneurial management of a firm's essential affairs, and the latter standing for line management below the board level with less charismatic, and more rational-legal traits. Therefore, the professional identity of management was under a double centrifugal influence:

(a) It was cross-cut by established identities like *Techniker, Bankkaufmann, Industriekaufmann*, etc.

(b) It was cut in half by perceived indenties of *Führung* and *Leitung*.

It would be too easy to explain this as the mere vestiges of a Teutonic authoritarian society organised along craft lines, reminiscent of the Middle Ages and out of date in modern society. For in one respect, nowhere else were there conditions equally advantageous to the emergence of management as a rather homogeneous profession: the legal structure of the *Aktiengesellschaft* (joint-stock company), introduced in the last century, provided for a separation of the inside and outside boards Anglo-Saxon style, the inside board (*Vorstand*) being composed of top managerial employees, not of directors elected by shareholders, running the firm as well as representing it to third parties. Thus, the first legal recognition of some sort of institutional autonomy of what was *de facto* top management, occurred in Germany. So why was Germany slower than Britain to accept the idea of 'management' as a professional group? I suggest that this was only to a small extent due to backwardness, or to a more distant cultural relationship with the USA. Instead, one has to look at how people are trained for managerial tasks, in order to explain why management means something different in Germany, and why people in that country are still hesitant to use this label.

The training background of German management

A short overview of relevant training institutions   Before giving any quantitative data on the training German managers have received, it seems appropriate to give a description of institutions, in particular insofar as they are different from British ones. German higher education consists of two tiers: universities and *Fachhochschulen*. There is a much more pronounced division of labour between them than in Britain between universities and polytechnics. Universities offer courses leading to a degree after four years of study as a minimum. In the context of this paper, relevant degrees are the *Diplom* which is at about the standard of a Bachelor's degree, but requires a larger area of knowledge to be studied and is less specialised; then there is the

D

Erstes Staatsexamen for lawyers, a state exam administered by High Court judges and professors. At this level, the standards of academic excellence are strongest.

Below the university level, the *Fachhochschulen* have a role comparable to the one originally assigned to the English polytechnics; they give training which is highly relevant vocationally, but not meant to conform to high academic standards. Thus, there is no teaching of 'pure' arts and sciences in *Fachhochschulen*, as there is in polytechnics. Courses usually last for three years, are full-time, and are offered for a range of applicants which goes beyond the grammar-school leavers, to comprise those who attended specialised higher vocational schools and had gained work experience. Degrees are about equivalent to the HND; they feature a *grad* (*graduiert*) component, which of course does not mean the same as 'graduate' in the English sense (*Betriebswirt grad, Ing grad*). *Fachhochschulen* are quite unlike polytechnics, in that they do not teach for university degrees, and deal with vocational training only. Consequently, there are no such things as external or CNAA degrees in Germany.

Returning to the universities, there is an important difference between technical and classical ones. Technical universities have a much more vocational bent than the arts or social science faculties, but also the natural science faculties of the classical ones. Their courses follow the pattern of medical education in differentiating between two stages: in the first half of the course, the scientific foundation of a subject is laid, whereas in the second half, the emphasis is on vocational practice and the handling of artefacts to a greater extent than in English technological education, as A W J Chisholm has shown. Degrees are called *Diplom-Ingenieur* (*Dipl-Ing*) or *Diplom-Wirtschaftsingenieur* (after a mixture of mechanical engineering and business studies), to name the most important ones for manufacturing. Education in the classical universities, however, is more 'scientific' and has not got such a dominant vocational second stage as in the technical universities. The most sought-after degree in preparation for management here is *Diplom-Kaufmann* ('diplomaed commercial man', to choose an awkward but literal translation), and to a lesser extent *Diplom-Volkswirt* (economist). A certain number of lawyers is also considered for managerial positions by firms, as are *Diplom-Chemiker*, who usually hold a doctor's degree in addition, in chemical firms. The difference between *Dipl-Ing* and *Dipl-Kaufm/Dipl-Volksw* graduates is fairly important, the engineers being much more oriented towards the running, repairing and designing of things in industry; whereas there is a stronger emphasis on the manipulation of abstract symbols ('theory')

in business and economic studies. An intermediate position is occupied
by the education of chemists which is highly scientific, but carries a
higher measure of vocational relevance in the chemical industries where
its graduates are favoured for management careers.

Going back to the level of *Fachhochschulen,* it must be said that
these differences in vocational relevance do not exist here; a
Betriebswirt (grad) is just as oriented toward the running and organisation of commercial affairs in industry as an *Ing grad* is toward the
running and design of technical things. Again, there are also mixed
degrees (business + mechanical engineering), offered after courses of
studies in both subjects, in the shape of the *Wirtschaftsingenieur (grad).*

Often complementary to higher education, but also in lieu of it,
there is a substantial amount of training within industry in preparation
for managerial jobs, developed primarily after the last war. As education leading to a *Dipl-Kaufm* degree is often too abstract, most large
firms run traineeships or induction programmes, mostly for a year or
so, to prepare candidates for concrete circumstances in a firm or branch
of industry. Some trade associations are also active in this field; for
instance, the Iron and Steel Manufacturers' Association runs one year
courses to make business, economics and law graduates familiar with
operations in the industry. Often enough, firms recruit people straight
after A levels (*Abitur*), offering traineeships leading into lower
managerial positions, which however give good prospects of promotion.
But entry via traineeship, after A levels, is customary in the commercial
sector of firms only, and would be a rare exception in the technical and
production sector of manufacturing. In general, the trend nowadays
is in favour of the graduate entrant, if only because the supply of
graduates, particularly in business administration (*Dipl-Kaufm*), has
increased considerably, so that school leavers who set their sight on
management more or less automatically enter for courses leading to a
Dipl-Kaufm or *Betriebsw (grad)* degree before starting work, that is,
if they do not prefer to go into technical management first, and read for
an engineering degree.

The institutions covered so far are general institutions, in the sense
that, in future, one would be increasingly unlikely to find a manager
who does not hold one of the degrees so far mentioned, and/or has
served a traineeship or apprenticeship. Let us now move on to the
institutions in much more selective demand, the management centres.
First of all, they are much less integrated with higher education than in
England. English management centres are often part of universities,
or are at least attached to them in some way, and they tend to mix
together younger management students and mature students with

considerable working experience; degrees in management are conferred upon both groups. This is quite an unusual thing from the German point of view. For, in Germany, management centres:

(a) do not give degrees;
(b) teach people with work experience only;
(c) are outside the system of public higher education;
(d) try to introduce a greater amount of both hierarchical and functional selectivity for each specified course, which, in a greater number of cases than in Britain, would probably be more specialised.

It seems that courses in Britain more frequently tend to be 'generalist', and that the clientele served by each centre and course in Britain is more heterogeneous in many respects. It reminds one of the differences between the two countries concerning the systems of vocational education, with the former technical colleges in Britain having an enormous variety of students, ranging from the apprentice on a day-release or sandwich course to the aspiring engineer reading for an external degree. This 'egalitarian' trait seems to be reproduced in the management centres in Britain, but it is totally absent in those in Germany. There, it is traditional for each training institution to serve a clientele more rigidly defined in terms of formal education and work experience; arguments in favour of equality of opportunity tend to aim at opening up possibilities of climbing to the next higher rung on the training ladder.

The influx of new ideas on management techniques and theories in Germany from the USA, led to the foundation of quite a number of centres; but it should be borne in mind that this surge did not go quite in the same direction as it did in Britain. In particular, it was not much connected with the universities institutionally, with centres and universities each trying to carve themselves different slices out of the total demand for management training. More about the activity of management centres is reserved for a separate section of the paper.

A number of further institutions could be mentioned because numbers of managers passed through them, particularly *Praktiker* who did not receive training specifically meant for managers. But it is precisely for this reason that it was not supposed to start a management career, but rather left the attainment of a managerial position to be decided on more individual merits later on, that I propose to leave consideration of this training aside. It will also be clear by now that I have left out arts or other degrees in science; as the next section will show, they play only a rare and marginal role in managers' careers in Germany. Some of them may be important in very special areas; a physics graduate might, for instance, be found as manager of a uranium enrichment plant. But similar typical exceptions cannot be dealt with in this paper.

The training background in public higher education

There have been quite a number of studies on the composition of management, and on managerial careers. A very good survey of these is available in English, written by May. Many of them deal with board members only, and are therefore not considered here. The most detailed and methodically most reliable survey was done by Brinkmann. The managers he studies are distributed over various branches of industry, trade, insurance and banking, and they do not include personnel at the foreman level, nor supervisory board members (the equivalent of non-executive directors) or owner-managers. The size of the sample was about 20000 managers in 100 firms in *Nordrhein-Westfalen*, a state of a population of over 16 million, in which one of the principal industrial areas of Germany (*Ruhrgebiet*) is situated. This study allows the sector of manufacturing to be isolated from other branches of industry, which is very desirable in view of the topic of this conference. Of the 14221 managers who filled in questionnaires in manufacturing, 58 per cent held one of the degrees mentioned above, or in marginal cases a different one; 42 per cent thus were non-graduates. Those holding an engineering degree (*Dipl-Ing* or *Ing grad*) amounted to 39 per cent of all manufacturing managers, 18 per cent holding a *Dipl-Ing* and 21 per cent an *Ing grad* degree. Thus engineers with a degree form the most important part of the manufacturing sample. In Germany there is nothing comparable to engineers with purely professional qualifications, but a fair number of the non-graduates can be expected to be engineers in the sense of having work experience in the technical sector of firms, as well as formal technician and foreman qualifications.

The overwhelming importance of engineers with a degree is further illustrated by the fact that only 5 per cent of managers in manufacturing had business/economics degrees (*Dipl-Kaufm, Dipl-Volksw*) from a university. However, it is clear that their share must have increased since the study was made, to the detriment of the *Praktiker* (no degree at all) share, and to a lesser extent to the one of the engineers. 14 per cent held other academic qualifications; most strongly represented in this group are expected to be chemists and lawyers, with very small numbers of arts, sociology, etc, graduates.

It is quite interesting to break the sample down into the commercial and technical sectors of firms. In the *technical* sector, of course, engineering graduates are even more strongly represented than in general; at the level of executive directors, graduate engineers (*Dipl-Ing* or *Ing grad*) represent 97 per cent of respondents in that category, but even at the lowest level studied, 55 per cent are engineering graduates, with *Ing grad* dominating at 34 per cent.

Passing over to the commercial sector, it might be surprising for the British observer to note that 20 per cent of commercial executive board members are graduate engineers, 16 per cent of whom are *Dipl-Ing*. At the same level, 18 per cent of the commercial managers are business graduates, which appears a small percentage; and 28 per cent hold other degrees, primarily chemistry and law. At the lowest level of the commercial sector, the share of *Praktiker* is quite large at 76 per cent; but even there we find engineering graduates at 5.4 per cent, whereas business graduates put up 8.8 per cent, and those with other degrees 10 per cent. The percentage of business/economics graduates is highest at the level below the board; it is 16.8 per cent and thus probably demonstrates the fact that the expansion of business studies at the universities really started only after 1945, and that business degree holders are consequently somewhat less senior people than engineers. However, at none of the four levels differentiated by Brinkmann is the share of business graduates larger than that of 'other academic degrees' (chemistry, law, etc). And of course they have not even remotely captured the dominant position in the commercial sector which engineers with degrees hold in the technical sector. On the contrary, there is quite a considerable portion of engineers throughout the commercial departments, particularly at higher levels. Business graduates have so far not made a sizable impact, and it is right that May should blame this on the too 'theoretical' and abstract training at the universities, in business administration. More about this will be said in the following section of the paper. However, it is safe to expect that the share of business graduates who are now managers, often after having done some sort of traineeship, has increased over the last ten years, with the universities producing them in ever greater numbers. In the later sixties, the University of Cologne, for instance, was throwing them on the market to the tune of 500 per year, plus a quarter of this figure in economics. In addition, the *Fachhochschule* branches of business were only built up after the Second World War, and are now producing larger quantities of *Betriebswirte* (*grad*) who are well sought after by industry because of their vocationally relevant training.

To sum up: (1) Degrees are more frequent at higher levels, *Praktiker* at lower levels. (2) Engineering degrees are near obligatory for promotion in the technical sector, and are still strongly represented in the commercial one, especially at higher levels. (3) Business and economics degrees are not as well represented in the commercial sector as engineering degrees are in the technical sector; but their share is on the increase.

Teaching curricula at universities and *Fachhochschulen*

Knowing what degrees German managers hold does not necessarily imply much information on their qualifications in the sense that one does not know what kind of knowledge higher education instills in students, or what skills it produces. A description of curricula of studies leading up to the most important degrees could thus be helpful. This description should concentrate on subjects where teaching is different in Germany from Britain, or where curricula are in transition. In law studies and professional training, there are rather more substantial differences between the two countries, not only because laws are different; however, I will not go into this because the differences are not so much those of vocational relevance. The equivalents of British arts and science courses are not discussed either, because they play no important role at all.

It therefore seems appropriate to concentrate on the four most important degrees, two each at the two different levels (universities and *Fachhochschulen*), and also two each in the technical and commercial branches of higher education; finally, the hybrid courses in both technical and commercial education will be given a short mention. Information on a large number of curricula is conveniently available in a guide edited by a state commission on educational planning; this chapter draws on sections of this guide, *Studium und Beruf*.

Starting in the order of importance for manufacturing, with engineering courses, it can be seen that they are usually divided into two halves. In the first half, teaching comprises the scientific foundations of a subject, for instance, calculus, thermodynamics, physical experimentation, chemistry, descriptive geometry, for mechanical engineers, as well as a general treatment of the technical artefacts a particular branch of engineering deals with, plus training in more elementary trade skills, like machines drawing in mechanical engineering. In the second half of the course, there is a more detailed and specialised treatment of the workings and construction of the artefacts peculiar to the chosen branch of engineering. Here, the student has to decide in which technical area to specialise; he will devote most of the time in this second half to studying a speciality, like automobile, chemical, textile, thermic, aircraft, reactor, or marine engineering. Chairs at universities and lectureships at *Fachhochschulen* are specialised and designated along these lines. Especially in this second half, teaching has a highly practical bent, and can be compared to the professional training of teaching hospitals in Britain; it would comprise most of what professional engineering institutions here are supposed to co-ordinate after university studies in engineering have been completed.

Courses last for at least four years in universities in Germany, but usually take a year longer, and at least three years in *Fachhochschulen*. There is a substantial degree of overlap between university courses leading to a *Dipl-Ing,* and *Fachhochschule* courses leading to an *Ing grad*, the difference between them being less one of vocational relevance than of technical and academic sophistication. Industrial work experience is required before starting and/or during the first half of each course. *Ing grad* students have to have worked in a relevant branch of industry for at least one year, whereas *Dipl-Ing* students usually have to give proof of at least half a year's work before finishing the first half of the course. *Ing grad* students on the whole have more substantial work experience anyway, often being recruited from among the skilled workers.

Higher education for the commercial side of the enterprise, however, cannot be described for universities and *Fachhochschulen* alike, in one and the same passage. Curricula show a greater difference between the two institutions. Studies for the degree of *Betriebsw (grad)* are very much the commercial equivalent to those for *Ing grad*, in that they are closely geared to the practical requirements in industry. Again, students have to furnish proof of at least one year's work; they are traditionally recruited to a larger extent amongst those who had specialised commercial secondary education, and had already worked in banking, insurance, trade, or the commercial side of manufacturing. Teaching is acknowledged to prepare students adequately for handling the commercial techniques they will encounter when entering firms as prospective managers. There is also some teaching of economics, work psychology, economic history, etc, but this is very rudimentary and occupies a small part of the course. The emphasis is on subjects like accounting, auditing, work organisation, business financing, rationalisation, planning, business taxation, civil law, especially commercial law and social legislation, that is, either on practising techniques or acquiring knowledge of important institutions and regulations.

The training of students for *Dipl-Kaufm* in the universities is much less centred on commercial techniques, and emphasizes theory instead. Still, on the face of it, there remain some of the elements of training in the former *Handelshochschulen* (Colleges of Commercial Education). Particularly in traditional commercial centres like Cologne, Mannheim, Nürnberg, Frankfurt, Hamburg, there was a tradition of local authorities setting up vocational colleges to train the future commercial elite. Thus, the curriculum structure for studies leading to a *Dipl-Kaufm* resembles the one for a *Dipl-Ing*, in the first half: there, the emphasis is on accounting, mathematics, statistics, civil and commercial law, and a grounding in the theory of business administration and economics.

In the second half, however, the teaching of abstract theory is stressed beyond all proportions; here, the transformation of *Handelshochschulen* into departments of the classical universities shows its effects in the neglect of familiarity with useful 'social artefacts' and real-life decision-making. Still, students have to specialise in this second half to some extent, in banking, auditing, insurance, informatics, organisation, marketing, manufacturing management, taxation, transportation/traffic, or other similar subjects. It is here that a higher degree of vocational relevance is introduced, but this suffers from the persisting, crushing weight of abstract theory, glorified in the name of academic excellence.

There are indications that, with the tremendous increase in business students over the years, state governments are keen on making better use of the money invested in business and economics faculties, by pressing them to increase the vocational relevance of teaching. From personal experience, I would say that any business student who does not want to make a career in the university, already tries to prepare himself as best he can for the branch of industry he has chosen, by devoting most of his interests to special studies in 'banking, marketing, etc, whilst mugging up dead-wood abstract theory in the most time-saving way possible. Within the framework of these special studies, there is also a beneficial presence of managers in seminars, contacts of chairs with firms, and some recruitment of people from industry into professorships. As regards the recruitment of students, they often have work experience (at least half a year is usually required) and/or secondary education with an emphasis on commerce and economics. Sometimes, they are turned off by the stress on abstract theory, and one can only hope that this will be changed once reform of curricula gets under way.

Another course of studies, which seems to have great value, should also be mentioned. After the war, it was realised that engineers needed a thorough complement of certain business administration knowledge, in order to occupy some managerial functions, particularly in the planning and construction of costly investment in capital-intensive industries. The technical universities thus created a hybrid course leading up to the degree of *Diplom-Wirtschaftsingenieur* (economical engineer, literally), with about equal emphasis on mechanical engineering and business administration. These courses have proved a success in preparation for managerial decisions about, for instance, investment in the chemical industries, which depend not only on a familiarity with advanced equipment, but also on advanced methods of calculating the profitability of investment alternatives, and which need a skill of structuring new investment following economic considerations. In a number of technical universities, this hybrid course is provided in the form of a two-year business extension course (Aachen, Braunschweig, München), in others, teaching of engineering and business takes place simultaneously (Berlin, Darmstadt, Karlsruhe). Thus again, the technical universities proved rather more adept at structuring courses to suit the needs of working people, than the classical universities which tended to raise the academic excellence of business courses at the expense of relevance. Along with the universities, the *Fachhochschulen* also introduced similar courses at their level, leading to the degree of *Wirtschaftsingenieur (grad).*

The work of management centres

Management centres are a rather heterogeneous lot, in Germany. To say that they all provide continuous education and training for management, would be a statement of a mere truism. A common denominator of the centres has already been mentioned, albeit in a negative form: they do not give degrees, they run courses shorter than those for management degrees in Britain, and are set up outside the system of public higher education. Connections between the centres and the universities or *Fachhochschulen* are informal, through individual people only. But this is really all that the centres have in common. There are those that are very specialised in their intake and subject area, like for instance the *Verkaufsleiterakademie* (sales manager academy) in Frankfurt, and those that cater for a very widely defined clientele like the early-established *Baden-Badener Unternehmergespräche,* or the *Akademie für Führungskräfte der Wirtschaft* in Bad Harzburg which even aims courses at the higher civil service. There are centres originally sponsored by influential businessmen, chambers of industry and commerce, entrepreneurial associations, state governments, or university professors, in various combinations.

A well-known description of the centres, by Fiedler-Winter, deals with 24 of them. The average number of participants may be as low as 20 in some institutions. Courses or seminars may last for anything from a week-end to half a year. Centres may be extremely rigorous in the way they handle experienced adults, imposing a very tight schedule and homework, as well as conducting examinations; but they may also be set in a more relaxing atmosphere, frequently organising week-end meetings in which the social position of entrepreneurs in present-day society is discussed over a generous supply of cigars and cognac. Therefore, global data on numbers of participants would not tell anyone much about the role the management centres play.

There is a need for a more qualitative analysis of what the centres actually do, to get some sort of order into that mixed bag of institutions, and show people what their activity is all about. For this purpose, I propose a very crude, incomplete, and inductivistic typology of functions which management centres may serve. This is a very unsystematic and spontaneous result of thinking about how to survey the work of the centres, with an eye to national peculiarities. These functions could be grouped under four headings:

(a) Teaching general management principles: things like management by objectives, divisional versus functional organisation, staff-line relationships, organisational behaviour, human relations, leadership patterns, motivation, theories X and Y, etc.

(b) Higher management techniques: linear programming, operations research, management information systems, budgeting, financial planning methods, corporate business strategy, 'case method', etc.

(c) Widening of specialists' knowledge: familiarising specialists (like production engineers, accountants, salesmen) with activities, techniques and knowledge outside their speciality. Fores termed this a 'conversion process'; but I chose a different label because I want to avoid implying a necessary reversion from skills and knowledge acquired in previous training.

(d) Teaching special skills and knowledge: methods of personnel management, sales organisation, marketing, accounting, auditing, investment planning, data processing, workflow analysis and organisation, training services, commercial and labour law, etc.

It will be obvious at first sight that there is no exact dividing line between either of these categories and the others. There is an increase, from 1 to 4, in the concreteness of teaching, and a decrease in the degree of abstractness and of a strategic ambition of teaching. It is of course impossible to fit the work of individual centres neatly into either or several of these messy categories. But I have tried to slot a centre into either of these categories if it seemed to me, from the description in the Fiedler-Winter book, that it put a stronger emphasis on the respective training category.

The categories which receive emphasis in most cases, are 'higher management techniques' (15 centres) and 'special skills and knowledge' (13 centres). It should be noted that the latter bracket is filled, to a substantial extent, by centres which are expressly limited in teaching only one management speciality: there are three special marketing centres, one personnel work institute, a controller academy, a centre for automation, data-processing and computerised control, an academy for work organisation, an institute to develop creativity. Thus, about eight centres concentrate on a speciality, which is one third of those surveyed.

Next in the order of emphasis given, is the 'teaching of general management principles' (10 centres). But of course, these are not dominating courses, to the extent that other areas are neglected; no centre would emphasise general principles alone, stressing either higher management techniques or special skills and knowledge at least equally. Last, we have the 'widening of specialists' knowledge', which is stressed in four centres explicitly. It could of course be implicitly achieved in the fulfilment of other functions, too. But it seemed worthwhile to single out some institutions which are highly selective, in that they aim training at engineers, in order to prepare them for management tasks which are not specifically technical. It is perhaps significant that the centre with the most rigorous schedule should fall into this slot; the Hamburg Institute for Industrial Co-ordination specifically recruits managers who have to:

(a) hold a *Dipl-Ing* or *Ing grad* degree;

(b) have had at least two years of industrial experience, and hold a position of managerial authority, whilst, if they have more than seven years' work experience, they should at least be heads of department;

(c) have professional and human qualifications to take over leadership tasks, which has to be certified by the firm if the applicant is delegated by it.

A number of other, non-specialised centres also offer courses designed to introduce engineers to the commercial side of the enterprise. In general, the centres try to prove their marketing skills by offering courses tailored to the needs of specific applicants and managerial levels or specialties. Therefore, although general management principles are frequently taught and emphasised, it is doubtful whether the 'generalist' manager is the person that German centres aim to produce, when compared to those in Britain. The activity of the centres will no doubt help managers in Germany to do their job in a professional way, but this is still a far cry from 'management' as a unified profession in the fullest sociological sense.

A systematic interpretation of management training in West Germany

The whole system of management training in Germany is often evaluated as showing a 'management gap' in comparison with other nations, notably the USA. This view was pronounced in exemplary fashion by Booz, Allen and Hamilton, the consultants, who made a report on German management for the Federal Government. This reflects well what an enlightened Anglo-Saxon management consultant, imbued with professional consciousness, might feel when taking a look at German management. Some points the authors mention are well worth thinking about, as for instance the partial unwillingness to adopt some management techniques, and frequent authoritarian attitudes stifling initiative. But, as Hartmann pointed out in his critique, one has the impression that the authors indulge in the view that their own management culture is superior to the German one, quite beyond the possibility of grading one cultural system against the other in terms of effectiveness. It seems to be taken too much for granted that the idea of 'management' as a profession is necessarily valuable, that the teaching of general management principles is very useful, and that all those management techniques and structures are superior everywhere.

In this view, the internal logic of the German system is obscured, and phenomena are not interpreted within that particular logic. What then are the features of this system which distinguish it from others? There is, first of all, the notion that managers who are on the technical side of the enterprise, should hold some engineering degree, including production managers, of course. Thus, in manufacturing the best chances for promotion are given to those who have the best technical education because they will know best what is going on in the enterprise. A similar view holds for those who take the first step on the managerial ladder on the commercial side of the enterprise; they should also have a sound, sort of elevated-craft grip on what they are doing. Therefore, if there is an assumption that people ought to have a thorough grounding in a vocationally-oriented institution of higher education before starting on the managerial ladder, then it follows that they have to be trained in a specialism first; for the idea of 'general management' is nonsense at lower management levels. Consequently, the idea of management as a profession does not occur; instead, separate occupational identities of engineers, sales people, financial people, etc, are fostered.

Of course, it may become necessary to change these identities as an individual climbs the managerial ladder to the top; there has to be a conversion process without any doubt. The need for this is not denied in Germany, but many people have doubts about the applicability of the techniques of higher management they might be taught. They might find general management principles quite stimulating to talk about in the relaxed atmosphere of a centre, away from the rat-race, but they would wonder what use they can make of doctrines like management by objectives, theories X and Y, Harzburger Modell, or something else. They would often find they practise it already, or that their deviation from it is quite justified in view of more individual constraints. It is therefore understandable that managers do not really flock into general management courses; Winter suggested in 1973 that management education had entered a crisis in Germany whilst blossoming in a number of other countries. But it must be doubtful whether this should be criticised as a form of under-development as it is by her. German management is pretty well on the way to a state where most of its members will hold a university or *Fachhochschule* degree, either in engineering, business administration, chemistry, or to a lesser extent in law, economics, or physics. Managers who originated on the technical side of the enterprise traditionally were engineers with a degree, and commercial ones increasingly will be business graduates. This being the case, and bearing in mind the doubtful value of general management principles and techniques, the functions of management centres could sensibly only be:

(a) to make engineers more familiar with the commercial side of firms;
(b) to improve the knowledge and skills of *Praktiker,* ie those who had little or no formal training;
(c) to fill the lacunae left by the classical universities through their heavily abstract-theoretical education in economics/business administration;
(d) to keep managers generally up to date on new methods, regulations, markets and equipment.

Hence there is the tendency, mentioned above, for German management centres to specialise; they would do well to remember that this makes them more viable in the long run, when the trendiness of present general principles will have faded. It is often deplored in

Germany that top management is unwilling to go to general management courses, and does not consider entrepreneurship as something that can be taught. But I wonder whether this is a particular German trait, or whether it is not the same in Britain, too. These top managers would be the ideal consumers of general management knowledge, yet they seem less willing to buy it from the centres.

Would it not be sensible to suggest that the idea of management as a unified profession has been stretched to its limits? As I have tried to show, the 'general management' uniform has always been cracking at the seams in Germany, and it seems that it has to come apart to some extent in Britain, too. This at least is a conclusion Stewart drew from her detailed study of managerial roles; Glover's literature review comes to a similar conclusion. In any case, it must be highly doubtful whether general management training can be very helpful when it is not superimposed on a layer of better training in a specialism, notably in engineering for manufacturing managers.

References

Booz, Allen and Hamilton, 'Germany management: challenge and response', a pragmatic review with an appraisal by Heinz Hartmann, *International Studies of Management and Organisation,* Vol 3, 1973

Brinkmann G, *Die Ausbildung von Führungskräften für die Wirtschaft,* Wienand, Cologne, 1967

Bund-Länder-Kommission für Bildungsplanung und Bundesanstalt für Arbeit (ed), Studium und Beruf, *Informationen für Abiturienten und Absolventen der Fachhochschulen,* Aspekte-Verlag, Frankfurt, 1972

Chisholm A W J, 'Some comparisons of the engineering education and training systems of Britain and Continental Europe', paper for a I MECH E conference, 1976

Fiedler-Winter R, *Die Management-Schulen,* Econ, Düsseldorf/ Wien, 1973

—'Leitern, die nach oben führen', *Arbeit und Leistung,* Vol 6, 1973

Fores M, Note on the conversion process which engineers and industrial managers face, Department of Industry, 1976

Glover I, 'Managerial work, a review of the evidence', The City University, 1977

Hartmann H, *Authority and Organisation in German Management,* Princeton University Press, 1959

Hutton S P, Lawrence P A and Smith J H, *The Recruitment, Deployment and Status of the Mechanical Engineer in the German Federal Republic,* University of Southampton, 1977

May B, 'Social, educational and professional background of German management, a review of the literature', Department of Industry, 1974

Stewart R, *Managers and their Jobs,* Macmillan, 1967

Making things:
a psychologist's view

Liam Hudson
BRUNEL UNIVERSITY

The author is professor of psychology at Brunel University. When this paper was written, he was professor of educational sciences at the University of Edinburgh. The paper has also been published in the journal *Crafts*

For nearly twenty years now, I have been caught up in one way or another with questions that surround the expression of human talent; with the routes that people follow in trying to bring their capabilities to bear in some satisfactory way on their work. You cannot watch such struggles for long without realising that the obstacles each individual faces are sometimes those of his own creation. It goes without saying that I am not the first psychologist in the world to notice these self-limiting and self-defeating properties of ours; and in passing would point to Otto Rank as someone who had shrewd things to say about the crises of self-sufficiency that each person must survive before he is free to perform his feats of 'will and deed'.

Specifically, Rank postulated a necessary conflict or tension between two sorts of fear: the fear of dependence and the fear of independence or isolation. And three stages in the resolution of this tension: (i) denial, in the form of adherence to totally conventional patterns of behaviour; (ii) conflict, in which we strike out on our own, but continually undermine our own efforts; and (iii) self-sufficiency, in which we are at last free to harness our warring emotions to some culturally significant purpose. Too neat, this scheme strikes me, nevertheless, as being on the right lines.

But it is not just our own fears that militate against us. Social attitudes and practical opportunities can militate too. And it is these more external constraints that bother me particularly at the moment. The young and talented in this country assume that it must be in some way demeaning to work for a living with your hands; and that making things, in a workshop or factory, is a boring business best left to others less fortunate.

It does not often cross the mind of a British undergraduate that factories can produce objects of real beauty; still less that he could help produce them. Factories are dirty places, he assumes, and commerce is morally compromising; while objects of beauty are produced by artists and craftsmen who work alone.

There is a gulf in other words, and a well-documented one, between what young people perceive as personally and aesthetically gratifying, and what they concede is socially useful. Between the prospects of felicity that exist in their imaginations, and the stark realities of earning a living. In other words again, industry has a 'bad image'. But such images do not spring into the adolescent mind from a clear blue void; nor are they created solely by sinister men in advertising agencies and television studios. To greater or lesser extent, they are earned. And once in existence, they create cycles of self-fulfilling prophecy, in which what is seen as depressing becomes depressing in fact.

I have argued elsewhere (Hudson and Jacot, 1971) that this malaise is conspicuously a British phenomenon; you do not find it in the same form in America, nor on the Continent of Europe. My view is that, in practice, it boils down to quasi-anthropological distinction between work that is 'clean', 'pure' and 'theoretical', as opposed to work that is 'dirty', 'practical' and 'applied'. And that this distinction in its turn is a residue of our historical fascination with the idea of a 'gentleman' (who does not carry parcels, let alone do manual work), and our distaste for money that comes from 'trade'.

But diagnosis is one thing, therapy another. So rather than help create a heap of evidence, all of which tells us how beleaguered we are, I want to attempt something more speculatively constructive. What I have in mind is an example or ideal type: an episode in our own industrial development from which luminous morals can be drawn.

This case takes us back in time past the mills that were dark and loathesome, and reminds us of the preoccupations that gripped William Morris: craftsmanship, pride in work, a human scale of working unit, and the marriage of skill with beauty. But far enough back, too, to shake off any hint of the worthiness that still hangs about Morris's name – to the England of the mid-eighteenth century, when our great cabinet-makers were getting into their stride, silversmithing flourished, and the manufacture of porcelain was in its infancy.

It is on porcelain that I want to concentrate: Chelsea porcelain. The antecedent history is probably familiar so I will sketch in only the outlines. During the seventeenth and eighteenth centuries, porcelain was being imported to Western Europe from China. Demand for it was voracious, and prices high; and although attempts to replicate the Oriental porcelain body were made repeatedly, they failed. The first successful approximation to it was reached at Rouen in 1673. But this French invention was artificial. Instead of mixing white china clay (kaolin) and china stone (putuntse), the French mixed the clay with ground glass. In comparison with the Chinese, this new 'soft-paste' body was awkward to handle in the kiln, frequently warping. On the other hand, it was of great beauty. Real 'hard-paste' porcelain was not made in Europe until 1709, when a German alchemist called Bottger produced some for his patron Augustus, the Elector of Saxony. A factory was established soon afterwards at Meissen. Meanwhile, the French continued to produce the artificial porcelain at St Cloud, and then at Vincennes and Sèvres.

Soon the secrets leaked, and other factories were set up on the Continent; but it was not until the early 1740s that news of the relevant techniques reached London – and, probably for reasons of proximity, it was the French method that was brought here rather than the German, the soft-paste rather than the hard.

The historical account of this dissemination centres on a coterie of Huguenot refugees then living in Soho. One of them, Thomas Briand, is said to have given a successful demonstration of a 'fine white ware' to members of the Royal Society in a Soho coffee-house in 1742, perhaps having brought the secret with him as a run-away workman from St Cloud. Soon after, in 1743, we hear of Briand joining together with two other French *émigrés* to set up a factory in Chelsea. His partners were Charles Gouyn, who seems to have provided the money, and Nicholas Sprimont, a silversmith.

The venture was an almost immediate success. But despite this, there were still troubles. Briand soon left, and then Gouyn dropped out too, leaving Sprimont as manager. Luckily, he found a new patron almost immediately, the Duke of Cumberland; and thereafter, from 1749 or 1750 onwards, Sprimont was effectively in sole control of the Chelsea works.

It is Sprimont who matters; Briand and Gouyn in comparison are shadowy and insignificant figures. But before I rehearse what we know about his influence, let us first be clear about the objects he produced. The style is *rococco*: that phase in the evolution of taste lying between the weighty authority of the baroque and the discipline of the neo-classical: light-hearted, poised – at worst vapid, at best much better than that.

Operating within this style or any other, the finesse of British craftsmanship rarely matched that of the French or German. But Chelsea porcelain of the red anchor period can stand comparison with any porcelain made. In terms of technique, it often verges on the rustic; but the cumulative effect is of an innocent vitality that neither Sèvres nor the German factories – Meissen, Nymphenburg, Berlin – ever quite equalled. Take, as an instance, the Chelsea product you are most likely to stumble across in a shop: a plate, decorated with flowers. The paste is lumpy, and the footrim has had to be ground smooth. But the sense of quality is unmistakable. And this despite the respects in which the piece is derivative. The porcelain body is an imitation of what was by now being done to the highest standards of technical excellence at Vincennes; and the shape and decoration are copied more or less directly from Germany; the style of Meissen's *Deutsche Blumen*. But especially when the decorators were on song, a red anchor Chelsea plate knows no superior: it is like a living presence in your hands.

How did it happen? The story turns on Sprimont, and what he achieved, he achieved astonishingly quickly. In 1742, when soft paste porcelain is heard of for the first time in England, Sprimont was twenty-six; having been apprenticed to his uncle, he had set up in business as a silversmith in Compton Street. By 1750, he was making the finest porcelain this country has even seen. And by 1756, when he was still only forty, the best days of the factory were over and done.

At 26 he knew little or nothing about making porcelain; by 40 he had finished making the best we possess. To put the same point less personally, our most beautiful porcelain was made within a decade and a half of the first germ of technical insight reaching these shores. In the two centuries since, there has been an enormous quantity of the stuff produced, but almost all of it is in comparison lifeless.

As soon as Sprimont was in effective control of the factory the flow of works of superlative quality began. But why did it stop, and so soon? One explanation, a profoundly important one I suspect, concerns the relation of creative enthusiasm to technical risk. It seems that a necessary, although insufficient, condition for the manufacture of beautiful objects is that the manufacturer's grasp of technique should remain experimental and in some degree precarious. Once the technique is mastered and becomes a matter of routine, the crucial element of challenge is lost and atrophy sets in.

But granted this quite general relation of technical risk to aesthetic quality, which holds, I believe, as much for motor cars as it does for porcelain, or cabinet-making, or the design of coins, other causes make their contribution. In Sprimont's case these are instructive. The first is that, in 1756, he fell sick. He had recovered by 1758, but there had been a two year hiatus; and thereafter, the nature of the Chelsea factory was changed.

When Sprimont returned from the spas, he introduced a new body, in which there were additions of bone ash to make it more tractable. He also introduced a new style. Where the red anchor wares combined a German style with a French body and created something unique, the new gold anchor wares were French in inspiration, both in body and style. And, sadly, were a provincial echo of what was being done with consummate skill, if dubious taste, at Sèvres.

Sprimont's health continued to decline. In 1763 he was gravely ill, and tried to sell up but failed. The sale was not made, in the end, until 1769. After a year's delay, the effects of the Chelsea factory passed *en bloc* into the competent hands of William Duesbury, and were taken off to Derby – at a cost to Duesbury of £600. Sprimont died in 1771, aged fifty-five.

Heavy-footedly, let me summarise. There are four points I want to make. One about the relation of scale to function; one about Sprimont's position as an outsider; one about his lack of relevant training; and one, in amplification, about creativeness and risk.

The point about scale is obvious and I will not labour it. Sprimont was a prime mover of real talent, and was fortunate to live in an age, whatever its shortcomings, when firms could grow, not for bureaucratic reasons, but to express a prime mover's vision. At a guess, I would say he employed upwards of 100 men; and when he was ill, many of them moved round the corner to his competitors at Bow. I am not implying that his was a one man band; far from it. He employed remarkable decorators like O'Neale, the fable printer, and gave them their heads. But the enterprise was organic in the sense that it existed, growing and then shrinking, as the vehicle for a gifted manufacturer's imagination. One can't help wondering, nervously, what would have become of Sprimont today; whether, like his natural heirs the artist-craftsmen, he would have preferred to work alone rather than cope with a small firm's paperwork.

On the question of Sprimont's status as an outsider, I would like to pause a shade longer. There are at least three issues here, and I do not know quite how to disentangle them. We know, at the level of common sense, that every human collectivity develops its own orthodoxies. It follows, as a matter of course, that innovations are easiest perceived by people who are in some way or other marginal. This is as true in molecular biology as it is in manufacturing raincoats.

So far, so good; Sprimont was an *émigré* and marginal by definition. But innovations, even great ones, often consist in recombinations of knowledge and skill: in the transposition of what is already known from old contexts to new ones. Granted this, *émigrés* not only have the ability to perceive how such shifts can be made, but are well placed, in terms of their contacts and mobility, to carry critical items of knowledge from place to place. Add to this a heightened desire to carve a niche for themselves and their families in their new society and the relation of the *émigré* to innovation becomes over-determined in a complex way.

Next, Sprimont's conspicuous absence of experience as a potter. Nowadays, we would expect to put someone through three years in a college of art, and add specialised postgraduate training in ceramic techniques, before expecting any significant contribution to be made. Yet Sprimont put down his silversmithing tools, took up the porcelain manufacturer's moulds, and after a few years' exploration, themselves conspicuously successful, achieved a higher standard of excellence than anyone before or since. The inference is that the protracted trainings we now require of any young person before he undertakes a skill, whether as a doctor, or engineer or PT instructor, serve functions other than those of inculcating skill.

Such trainings account for massive quantities of our gross national product, so allow me to dwell a little. Doctoring is a helpful parallel. Although a medical student labours for many years to qualify, he is given little experience in any of those medical skills he will practice day by day – whether as a specialist or as a general practitioner. And if he is a GP, he will probably meet and diagnose many of the common ailments almost for the first time on the job. Further, he will have been encouraged to see these common complaints (and especially any that are psychological or psycho-somatic) as trivial compared with what occurs in hospital: radical surgery and specialised physical diagnosis. In other words, his training is not just long, but in some ways actively maladaptive.

Medical training is not alone. Our school-teachers are trained at length and eventually certificated, having learnt some second-hand psychology and social science, but having been told little about the most primitive skill they will need to perform: maintaining, order. And consider the training of army officers. Great attention is paid, on both sides of the Atlantic, to drill. But the aspiring young officer learns little of the critical moments that lie ahead when he tries to exercise his authority. My own experience as a National Service subaltern seems to have been characteristic. I developed great expertise at drill; enough to take part in the Coronation parade. But was once set out totally unprepared, with a gun and a small squad of men, to break the petrol tanker driver's strike in the London Docks. It was an amiable occasion, and we were ineffectual. But had it not been amiable, I would have had no syllable of instruction about how to cope. On another occasion, I set out as orderly officer to arrest a man who had found his wife locked in a lavatory with a male colleague, and was threatening murder. I did not know how to arrest someone; nor what to do if he resisted. At the humblest level, I did not know what noises should come out of my mouth. Happily, the potential assassin helped me out; but what if he had not?

Although gestures are made towards the fashioning of relevant skill, this is not undertaken seriously. I can only conclude what any sane observer must conclude. That if vocational training is not a species of disguised unemployment, it must be a process concerned to mould the recruit's identity – gradually to create in his mind a sense of membership or caste. If the Chinese can train medical auxiliaries in months to perform the skills that our GPs perform, why else do we allow medical training to last so long?

And what, nowadays, would we have expected of Sprimont? A vocationally oriented course at university, followed by postgraduate experience in a business school? One cannot help feeling that while this recipe would suit those of us who make our livings in higher education, it is one that we, like the Chinese, would be wise to resist.

Finally, I would like to say something more about the stimulating effects of technical risk. Vitality, it seems, has a shortish span, and I have suggested that this is so because techniques are mastered and become boring. But vitality has other roots; there are other sorts of tension for the prime mover to resolve. Let me suggest where one of them lies.

Unfortunately, we seem to know little about Sprimont as a person, and little about his decorators. But, via his journals, we do have access to another of these talented china painters: a much younger man, Quaker Pegg, who worked for William Duesbury's son at Derby. He is an intriguing soul, and worth mentioning, because he reminds us of where we began: with the notion of creative work as the symbolic resolution of private unease.

Pegg was born to humble parents in 1775. From an early age, he seems to have lived immersed in a potent Calvinistic melancholy. At the age of twenty-one, he went to work in the Derby factory as a decorator, and established his reputation as a painter of flowers. Now, flower-painting on porcelain is a highly stylised art. And at Derby this was as true as anywhere else. The remarkable thing about Pegg's flowers – and he seems to have painted nothing else – is that they are both naturalistic and sumptuous. At their best, they spread across the plate, petal on petal, like a declaration of the Pleasure Principle: a treat to behold.

But Pegg was so upset by the dissonance between the sensuality of his own products and his religious principles, that he gave up painting, and went instead to make silk stockings. However that too made him uneasy, as he records, because 'the hose were more for show than use'. He says that he 'often blush'd with guilt' when he reflected on it; as wrong in its way as painting. So he moved to making cotton stockings instead, finding this less compromising. But even then ornamental 'clocks' were required of him. In the end he says: 'I prevailed on my employer to let me make the stockings without the clocks, and that gave me some relief'.

After some years of unswerving rectitude, the demands of conscience seem to have subsided, and at thirty-eight he returned for a while to Derby and to his flowers. He even married. But a few years later, his eyesight failed, and that was the end of that.

A sad story, but enough, I hope, to rebut any suggestion that our factories should be thrown open to the young and Dionysian. My view, on the contrary, is that manufacturing remains an activity of special excitement – and even, sometimes, of aesthetic significance – only as long as its prime movers are gifted, and are caught up, neck and crop, in surviving some intrinsic risk that it poses. I am making no assumption about the prime mover's level of grandness. Sprimont was a man of influence, but Pegg remained humble and idiosyncratic; yet both made an impact of cardinal significance by means of the objects they left behind them.

At the moment there is a remarkable renaissance of craft skill in this country. All around us, potters, weavers, jewellers, carpenters, glass blowers are practising their crafts at levels of technical expertise that, even a few years ago, would have been thought extraordinary. Many have had trainings at colleges of art; but most would see any solid commitment to industry or commerce as tantamount to selling their souls – a species of defilement. It seems to me sad and even shocking that this split between craftsmen and industry should be taken so totally for granted.

Black has recently commented on the spirit of nihilistic exploration that characterises much of the work now being done in colleges of art – a symptom, I would suggest, of the colleges' dislocation from a proper industrial base. The recent efforts of art students in Leeds are one instance among many: each son of toil his own Dada!

Elsewhere, in Scandinavia for example, no such radical separation exists: there are solitary craftsmen, massive industrial concerns, and any number of half-way houses in between. And as a result, their products often have a coherence that we can only envy: not flashy 'styling' superimposed on manufactured goods, but objects from the hands of engineers who have taste and respect for craftsmanship, and from craftsmen who have an understanding and respect for engineers.

In any society worth working in, this must surely be so. Men like Sprimont and Pegg should still have elbow-room in which to deploy their gifts. We should have small factories on the scale of the Chelsea works; colleges of art housing research and development units for the pertinent industries; art students working on industrial sandwich courses; artist–craftsmen working in industrially sponsored studios – all these forming bridges between elements of our society that are at present split apart. You might object that a man like Sprimont was interested in making money. But why not? – as long as it did not lead him to believe that his porcelain factory was something of which he ought to feel ashamed.

References

Atkinson P, *An Ethnography of Medical Education*, Unpublished PhD thesis, Edinburgh, 1976

Black M, 'The axe or the adze', *Crafts*, July 1976

Dixon J L, *English Porcelain of the 18th Century*, Faber, 1952

Honey W B, *German Porcelain*, Faber, 1947

—*French Porcelain*, Faber, 1950

Hudson L, 'The stereotypical scientist', *Nature*, Vol 213, p 228, 1967

—and Jacot B, 'Education and Eminence in British Medicine', *British Medical Journal*, Vol 4, p 162, 1971

—'The limits of human intelligence', in *The Limits of Human Nature* (ed Benthall J), Allen Lane, 1973

—*Human Beings*, Cape, 1975

—'Life as art', *New Society*, 12 February 1976

Lucie-Smith E, *The World of the Makers*, Paddington Press, 1975

McClelland D C, 'The calculated risk', in *Scientific Creativity* (eds Taylor C W and Barron F), Wiley, 1963

MacKinnon D W, 'Personality and the realisation of creative potential', *American Psychologist*, Vol 20, 1965

Pye D, *The Nature and Art of Workmanship*, Studio Vista, 1971

Savage G, *18th Century English Porcelain*, Spring, 1964

Stoller R J, *Perversion*, Harvester, 1976

Professionalism and manufacturing industry

Ian Glover
THE CITY UNIVERSITY

The author is on the academic research staff at
The City University

The thesis that the running of units in British manufacturing needs to be more 'professional' has been advanced with increasing frequency for at least a century and a half. By 'professionalism', most of the proponents of that point of view simply meant competence; so to argue that advocacy of this prescription has helped to frustrate its own aim is rather like arguing in favour of sin. Yet it has done this, because such advocacy has too often been allied to misunderstanding of the requirements of executive work in manufacturing, and of the best ways of producing able people to do it.

In practice, 'management professionalism' has been associated with a description of jobs that overemphasises their static, observational and clerical elements. It has sought to justify itself by stressing what turns out to be an idiosyncratic conception of the use of science, and by stressing the idea that the professional person shows a special sense of responsibility to society. It has been concerned, as well, with the status of job-holders, rather than with their performance.

Professionalism turns out to be a unique idea to Britain among the European countries. Partly-equivalent Continental terms, *métier* and *Beruf* place much more emphasis on activity and skill, and much less on a connection with a body of knowledge and on preoccupation with the job-holder's status. Professionalism has acted, in fact, as a buffer between the worlds of education and industry, producing unnecessary proliferation of cosy service occupations, of qualifications, and of interests to be consulted whenever changes are mooted. Moreover, it has helped to seduce able young people away from jobs in manufacturing which are more directly useful and challenging, than some of those that have been fully 'professionalised'.

Executive work in manufacturing

The 'classical' view of the role of the senior executive is that his job is to plan, organise, co-ordinate, and control. According to this view he is a 'decision-maker', much concerned with the flow and rational use of 'hard' information, with relationships amongst job-holders, with organisation and position in the hierarchy. In many key respects, this view is a convenient fiction.

The social-scientific literature on the work of those who manage resources can be criticised for having failed to study work in a comprehensive way; this is because an exaggerated concern with relationships between job-holders has led to neglect of the study of work output and work content: see, for instance, my literature review. Further, cultural and historical factors, which influence the ways in which jobs have been created and performed, have been devalued in importance and sometimes misunderstood. In spite of this, however, and in spite of some fairly obvious disciplinary and other biases on the part of those who have studied executive work, the literature does help to show that such work is not sensibly conceived in 'classical' terms.

Carlson was one of the first to doubt the sense of the classical view. His pioneering research, conducted in the late 1940s, made it clear that, for chief executives, there was an 'ideal' day which contrasts with a 'typical' one. For his sample, the amount of time they spent on problems which they misclassified as abnormal, left them without enough time to plan and reflect. So there were gaps between what the subjects thought they were doing, what they said they were doing, and what they were really doing.

All of these points suggest agreement with a more recent view of Mintzberg that 'there is . . . no science in managerial work', and that its main characteristics include variety, fragmentation, and brevity. Virtually all research into the nature of executive work, from the 1950s to the latest work of Stewart and her team, supports this conclusion. A number of general conclusions are suggested by this research, when it is put together with supporting evidence about executives and their employing units.

First, the jobs that executives do are diverse in the extreme, varying according to functional specialism, occupational background, level in the hierarchy, the nature of employing units, the products or services provided, and a very wide range of social and cultural influences. This fact alone does not augur well for those who wish to make generalisations about 'managers', or for those who imply that the executive gives up his specialism when anointed with 'management' status.

Second, executive work is distinguished by its largely unprogrammed character. Executives have responsibilities, while subordinates perform tasks; so the local environment of the job is ambiguous, virtually by definition. Lack of information is normal, especially 'hard' information of a kind potentially relevant to the job. Much of that which is available to the executive is distorted or incomplete, increasingly so in more and more complex and turbulent environments.

Third, studies employing observation and diary-keeping have shown the pressurised, often-interrupted and predominantly verbal character of executive work. Short, informal conversations are the norm; in 1957, Burns found that executives spent up to 80 per cent of their time in this way. Only 10 per cent of the tasks of the chief executives in Mintzberg's study lasted more than an hour; half lasted for less than nine minutes.

They were constantly disturbed from scheduled tasks. Face-to-face, verbal encounters were preferred to paperwork: networks of contacts were crucial to the job. Executives were 'not reflective planners, but adaptable information manipulators who prefer the live concrete situation'. A typical remark overheard was 'I don't want it good. I want it Tuesday'.

The characteristics of holders of middle-level jobs and their work have been shown to differ consistently from those of top job-holders. Attitudes to work and towards other groups are influenced greatly by the nature of the individual's specialism. Conflicts between members of different functional specialisms are normal. Specialist information is a major weapon and a major source of power *vis-à-vis* superiors, colleagues and subordinates. The working, and other, concerns of middle-level people have a more current, specific and short-term character than those of top job-holders. Finally, while the literature focuses much too heavily on relationships, and on the so-called 'managerial' aspects of executive work, it is clear that functional specialisms vary considerably and systematically with regard to skills demanded. Production executives are trouble-shooters; personnel men more concerned with documented information; and so on.

Another general feature of all executive jobs concerns the process of decision-making. This turns out to be far more political, irrational, and lengthy than the advocates of a 'scientific' kind of executive work would wish. Every conceivable type of personal, social and cultural factor can intrude, and rightly so. Attempts to study the process seem overly academic; attempts to 'programme' it are seen to be like the search for fool's gold, confusing the academic ball-game of analysis with the executive's task of synthesis.

In fact, the typical executive simply does not appear to do the kind of work that the management literature wants him to. Rather than being primarily a decision-maker and a planner, he is an inspirer, a fire-fighter, and a rationaliser after the event. His motives tend to be private and unpredictable, his thought-processes intuitive. His skills are largely specific to his unit; in production to details of the process and product: in sales, to details of the product. Further, they are literally unknowable to the observer-scientist, who can only record what he sees. The more successful the executive is at wielding resources, and at making things happen through entrepreneurial acts of synthesis, the more difficult will it be for the outsider to apprehend the personal skills and 'flair' being employed.

To sum up the argument so far, executive work in manufacturing aims to make and sell three-dimensional artifacts. To make artifacts, use is made of knowledge of many kinds, some of which will normally be of the public, scientific type; but much more use is made of detailed, personal, and product-specific information and skill. Because so much of this information and skill is private, it is extremely difficult, indeed probably pointless and largely impossible, to analyse its use within a conventional scientific tradition.

The liberal professional

In eighteenth-century England, any kind of occupation could be called a profession; skilled trades were called 'mechanical professions', for example. Outside the armed services and government, 'divinity, physic and the law' were virtually the only occupations regarded as suitable for a gentleman; they were the 'liberal' or learned professions. Nowadays, the accent on specialised training is far greater, but the feeling for a gentlemanly status and life style remains.

Most of the considerable literature on the modern Anglo-Saxon professions argues that an occupation is only professional if it can relate to a particular body of knowledge or science. There is a 1:1 connection between a body of knowledge and an occupation, to underpin claims that certain jobs should be done by members of the group. Also the 'professional' group is expected to project a certain sense of responsibility to the society in which it lives. Finally, it has to be a discrete group with definable boundaries for its work, and with members using a specific set of skills, whose use is exclusive to themselves.

The professional group is, in fact, partially a self-governing one. It sets its own standards in the same way that the guilds were given power to do by the medieval state: controlling entry itself, and exercising discipline on its members. One of the most frequently cited of numerous lists of attributes of a profession is that of Greenwood. The main elements are:
(a) a basis of systematic theory, based on rationality and self-criticism as opposed to traditionalism;
(b) professional authority, derived from (a) and located in the 'functional specificity' of his knowledge over the layman's ignorance;
(c) the sanction of the community, with power to licence its members, and privilege of confidentiality over dealings with clients;
(d) a regulative code of ethics, both formal and informal; and
(e) a professional culture derived from the values and norms of service, which govern the action and the symbols of the occupation.

As Roth tellingly points out, these attributes rarely coincide in practice, and are best understood as mere 'claims for . . . control and autonomy'.

The archetypal professional is the lawyer or doctor. His origins are those of a small-town big shot from eighteenth century, pre-industrial life. He is usually an adviser, or a consultant. He provides a service, not a good. His work tends more towards that of a clerk than an entrepreneur, in the sense that his output very often takes the form of a report of some sort written on paper. His clients and his peers rate his output as much by elements of rectitude, such as rightness or truth against a scale, as by market criteria such as utility, price and date of delivery.

Most academic discussion of the nature of the Anglo-Saxon professions have been conducted by sociologists, who have recently become more critical of the claim to a special degree of social responsibility. Yet the same commentators have failed to note, and to emphasise, the point that modern professions are mainly Anglo-Saxon constructs. They have also failed to appreciate major differences between Anglo-Saxon and Continental European conceptions of work and skill. The idea of *métier*, combines English-language ideas of skill and occupation. It does not refer to social status: the law provides a *métier*, but so do the jobs of the baker and cabinet-maker. More than either of the English terms, profession and occupation, *métier* implies diligent use of personal skills. A rather similar German term, *Beruf*, also suggests the use of skill in varied and complex tasks, and a sense of useful vocation. Incidentally, the second English term, occupation, suggests the process of watching the clock betweeen tea-breaks; whereas the person with a *métier*, or a *Beruf*, might be expected to enjoy his job a good deal more.

Professionalism and manufacturing: the mismatch

As I have argued, executive work in manufacturing is primarily concerned with making and selling three-dimensional artifacts. The work of the typical professional person, in contrast, belongs to the economist's service sector and its output normally consists of advice, very often in a two-dimensional paper form. The work of the executive stresses activity and skill; that of the professional is closer to science and observation.

As noted above, one of the main general characteristics of a profession revolves around the idea of direct responsibility to the local community. Professional conferences, journals, ethical codes, and offers of advice are conspicuous, by their presence and their usefulness in enabling professional groups to 'do well by doing good'. In the general setting of increasing division of labour and a growing service sector, the scope for this feature of professionalism mushrooms. Yet for the executive in manufacturing it is, at best, unnecessary.

His unit will stand or fall mainly by its ability to satisfy its customers. Even when the executive is a finance or personnel man, and so not directly concerned with the product, the notion of responsibility to a group of professional peers is not as relevant as it is in the case of the doctor or the lawyer. If the executive does his job effectively and legally, people outside his unit should be happy just to let him carry on. The manufacturer is only responsible to the local community in an indirect way, through running a decent operation.

I have already mentioned a more important feature of the mismatch between the professional depiction of work and manufacturing: a tendency to emphasise the observational, static and clerical element as against the normally more important elements of activity and skill. This emphasis is based in part on the idea of the 1:1 relationship between a body of knowledge and a 'professional' group. Use of a special body of knowledge, relatively inaccessible to those outside the group, implies the existence of trade secrets, and of conflict with the basic scientific principle that the scholar's knowledge should be available to all.

So the stress on the esoteric, implied by claims to professionalism, tends to elevate the scholarly and clerical part of the range of tasks performed by group members. It helps to define members of the higher occupations as those wearing white collars, sitting at a desk, writing reports from time to time, communing with a scientific muse. Professionalism is knowledge-specific, with members given special powers of understanding by science.

Most jobs do not fall into the 1:1 occupation to science pattern; they rely instead on many types of knowledge and information, with a great deal of it being completely different from the type that comes from the academy. Executive work, well conducted, invariably needs to draw on more than one science; the production man needs to know some psychology, the personnel man some physics, etc. However, most of the information which executives seek is not scientific at all, consisting instead of private information, or hunches about people, products or markets. They are interested in what will work in a given and unique situation; they are less interested in elegant analysis, universal principle, or the 'truth'. Executive work is best conceived of as being skill-specific, rather than knowledge-specific; knowledge, skill and experience are all necessary, none exclusively or even predominantly.

E

Another way in which professionalism has been imperfectly matched with the needs of manufacturing, one perhaps more directly observable than the last, is through proliferation of occupations. For over a century, British occupational groups that were socially above the salt have been allowed to run their own affairs, particularly to take on the qualifying function and, through this, control the numbers of qualified people. The arrangement has permitted some flexibility over qualifications, some social mobility of a kind, and a certain openness of expression. At the same time, however, it has produced a middle class whose forms of collective organisation are fragmented in the extreme, and whose attitudes to knowledge and occupations remain to a large extent medieval. It has also presented governments with a large number of long-established groups to be consulted whenever change is mooted.

Attitudes towards careers, as well as attitudes to work and skill, have suffered through professionalism. Proliferation of qualifications, those obtained after the individual's full-time education is over, tend to make him look around continually and over his shoulder at potential rivals, when he should be focusing on the job in front of him. Along with the continued high status of sedentary types of work, this means that the individual is always thinking of promotion as something to be achieved through adding more letters to his name, and through a conspicuous exhibition of 'theoretical' types of understanding, rather than through diligent performance of the task in front of him.

In manufacturing, the effect of professionalism leads to an elevation of 'service' jobs at the expense of those in production and sales. And ambitious individuals with lower middle-class origins, who feel that they lack the social skills needed for top jobs, become mobile 'spiralists', or 'cosmopolitans', depending on their professional peer group for their identity. In this way, they are less loyal than they ought to be to the needs of their units and to those who work with them.

In itself, proliferation of occupations is sometimes quite remarkable in Britain. We have, according to interpretation, about forty types of 'professional' engineer, whereas it is reasonable to argue that there are only two or three in Continental countries. The nature of the training and means of specialisation of British engineers are much less skill-specific than those of their Continental European counterparts. Yet, at the same time, British engineers are not trained and selected in ways that fit them to be top job holders. There are also three main types of accountant in the UK, effectively none on the Continent, where financial jobs are undertaken by more broadly-educated commercial and financial specialists.

It should be noted too that, whereas engineers and accountants perform two of the main roles in manufacturing, other occupations and functions have proliferated on a similar pattern. There are three types of quantity surveyor in Britain, for example, none on the Continent. Head office specialists, especially those in the 'management services' area, are more in evidence here than elsewhere in Europe.

It is fairly obvious that British manufacturing has suffered for a century or more through the attractiveness of the professions for the able young. The professions provide them with a cosy *demi-monde* between the academy and the world, one which leans on connections with the academy, and which, by implication, does not demand too much hard work. As we shall see, Continental institutions and customs do not provide this cosy world.

The second point is very important. Because British higher education has not been given the key responsibility for qualification, and for providing the more vocational element in the full education of people like engineers, education tends to be out of touch with work. Among broadly-equivalent Continental institutions, those that teach obviously-vocational subjects have had this responsibility for many decades. Also, Continental industrialists and academics tend to talk more with a common language, and courses adopt much more closely than ours the requirements of jobs and employers. Chisholm has observed:

'Of vital importance is that fact that in most Continental countries it is still considered almost essential to have for the teaching of engineering practice in the senior parts of the courses, professors who have actually practised as senior engineers and have been responsible for engineering works. These engineer-professors have had effective control of academic policy, unfettered by the possibly different aims and values of other academic disciplines'.

It is reasonable, of course, that doctors and lawyers should be versed in the secrets of medical and legal studies, and try to show a special sense of responsibility towards society. A member of any highly skilled occupation needs academic study as a part of his training and education; and services provided by independent occupations are not easily monitored by the market mechanism. But in manufacturing, scientific principles and other laws handed down from the academy are often unimportant in the tasks facing executives. They are useful only as background information, as distinguished from the complicated mass of practical details of products, markets, and people with which the executive has mainly to deal. Ethical codes and principles have a similar role. Both types of principle, scientific and ethical, are less useful than the outsider might imagine.

'Management professionalism': origins and attractions

According to Wilensky the suggestion that executives in industry might form a profession, or exhibit features of professionalism, 'has been taken out and dusted for decades'. To consider further the attractions of management professionalism, a brief historical treatment needs to be provided.

The modern Anglo-Saxon social institutions and ideologies, that the term 'professionalism' encapsulates, owe their origins to two notable features of eighteenth-century English society. One of these was the social standing of overseas trade, which by virtue of an association with politics and government and the success of those who undertook it, was distinctly higher than any trade or commerce that took place internally. The merchant princes who dominated overseas trade were often as rich as the greatest landed proprietors whose values still dominated society. From the eighteenth century onwards, overseas trading continued to be linked with military and political activity abroad, helping to keep the eyes of dominant political and financial interests averted from manufacturing at home. This was a part-cause of a powerful British tradition of an arms-length stance towards manufacturing. According to this tradition, dirty work in factories was for the lesser breeds.

Another notable feature of eighteenth-century England was the attitude towards social mobility. While society was hierarchical, it was more mobile than was the case in most other 'modern' European countries. A man could buy himself into the aristocracy, hence into power, in a way that was hardly possible in other parts of Europe. The ultimate beneficiary of these features of eighteenth-century society was the old aristocratic landed interest. The tradition of sanctioning a certain amount of social climbing gave the successful manufacturer of later years a social goal to which he could reasonably aspire. Along with the attitudes towards overseas trade, it also favoured political stability in a more general sense. In an even more general sense, of course, the imperial distraction was a pervasive factor delaying adaptation to the institutional and cultural requirements of a modern industrial society.

Because of all these, and other, factors, it is fairly reasonable to argue that Britain's economy turned into an industrial one too early and too slowly to help force through a social revolution of the kind which occurred in other countries, and in which whole aristocracies vanished. Nineteenth-century British settlements, between the old ruling groups and the new manufacturing and other interests, in education, government, politics, and elsewhere reflected the continued dominance, through that century and after, of essentially aristocratic attitudes towards occupations and the use of knowledge for practical ends. Knowledge was to be conspicuously consumed, not used as an input to the development of skill. Hard work was for the lesser breeds. None were keener to make such attitudes their own, than the middle-class *arrivistes*, amongst whom the new professional occupations must be counted.

The story of neglect of vocational education for manufacturing in Britain is now fairly well-known. The products of the public schools and universities were long socialised as potential custodians of a now-vanished Empire. The vacuum was inadequately filled by educational institutions of second-best status. Recently Kumar has discussed the history of the middle classes, and has pointed to the existence of three groups which form the modern middle class. The first, that of 'independent trading and manufacturing entrepreneurs', largely came to the fore between the late eighteenth and late nineteenth centuries. The second consisted of the new Victorian professional experts, both independent and salaried, solicitors, chemists, accountants, Veblen's engineers and Burnham's managerial elite, and so on. These evolved through the present century into Galbraith's 'technostructure', now mainly salaried employees in manufacturing, who have been attacked for their narrowness, and who 'willingly put their skills at the service of the Warfare State'.

The third group had come to the fore after 1945. These 'personal service professionals' consisted of highly qualified salaried employees in 'education, research, health, social welfare, social and public administration, planning'. In societies such as the USA, and especially Britain, with strong and partly justified traditions of mistrusting those who run their manufacturing base, the rise of this group helped to salve the 'moral' consciences and aspirations of important segments of the expanding middle class. Teaching of social science was expanded partly in order to provide those in the third group with their 'sciences', as argued on pages 119–123.

As Kumar rightly notes, members of the last two groups in Britain (the 'specialist' and the 'public service' professionals) strongly espouse traditional, idealised, 'professional' aspirations, especially for their children, while rarely experiencing their fulfilment. This is a function of their subordinate status at work, their individual experiences of upward social mobility, and of course, of the lingering power of the pre-industrial ideal of professionalism. Proliferation of competing occupations and confused political and administrative actions where education and industry come in contact are contemporary results of the historical events described above. It is at least arguable too, that the establishment in the 1960s of the so-called 'technological' universities and the manner of setting up the business schools can be regarded as expressions of the same confusion. In both cases, those who did not know enough about the nature of executive work seem to have hoped that 'science' would solve a manufacturing problem fairly directly.

The management idea

On the 'management' idea, the first point that should be made simply concerns the use of the term manager, which could easily be declared redundant. Just as most working 'technologists' turn out to be engineers by qualification and function, so do most 'managers' turn out to be specialists of one kind or another. Indeed, as was noted earlier in this paper, and as Child suggested in 1972, roles are so diverse that use of the term 'manager' is sensible only in the technical setting of the discussions of administrative and other social sciences. Also, as Fores and I have noted elsewhere, it is hard to see why executives in industry should not be classed as 'facing the same kinds of problem as theatrical directors, football managers, and prime ministers'; in reality 'each enjoys formal authority over a unit and needs to "run it" towards some end'.

The history of the 'management' idea in Britain has been one of self-justification and social aspiration. So it has been associated with claims to 'professional' autonomy and status, a heroic depiction of the job-holders' work and faith in a quantitative and decision-centred conception of management science. Part of the impetus behind it has undoubtedly also been towards greater efficiency and responsibility. But much of the rationale has been misguided: a product of a faulty Victorian specification of manpower needs.

What made the British management movement a viable possibility was Victorian neglect of higher vocational education and manufacturing. The development of management thinking *per se* began in the later decades of the nineteenth century under the influence of perceived national economic difficulty and employer paternalism. It was, however, above all, connected with the emergence and growth of a stratum of salaried executives.

In the interwar years, but especially after 1945, industrial social science highlighted the superficialities of 'management principles'. A wide range of social pressures undermined the movement's claims to legitimacy. So its concerns became increasingly practical as its academic side declined, or merged incoherently with social science, and as some of its detailed features were taken over by specialised interest groups. From Taylor, through Mayo, the post-war productivity teams, to management development, Herzberg, and the business schools, American practices were, as Mant has argued, studied and imitated. In many instances the imitation has been uncritical, involving neglect of key aspects that have contributed to the USA's relative success. The latter include, for example, that country's superior natural resources and its greater reliance on the mainly German work ethic of middle America. It is possible that the American version of the management idea was constructed to fulfil a rather different social need from the one it was constructed to fulfil in Britain. Ethnic, rather than class, barriers dominate in America. American 'management' seems to have been constructed in order to celebrate economic success, and as a leveller designed to provide a common culture by spicing the mixture in a melting pot which has been less successful.

Deschooling executive work

It is clear that the Continental system for matching education to work is more modern than the British one. At least, it is more fitted to the needs of societies in which manufacturing has become the dominant economic activity. What can be learnt from Continental practice? Which features of the British system might be retained or developed?

My other paper in this book has reported that executives in manufacturing in countries such as France, Germany and Sweden are better qualified, and in more relevant subjects, than is the case of their British counterparts. Without the existence of professional groups, higher education in those countries has taken a more direct and successful role in producing top job-holders than is the case for Britain. Engineering schools, and later undergraduate schools of business administration have been set up, for instance in France and Germany, in response to the needs of employment. This represents a rational, and successful, response to intensified competition in markets; and there has been no need for 'professional' qualifying associations to supplement the efforts of the state system: no buffer to be sited between education and manufacturing.

To answer the first of the questions posed, the claim is not so controversial that the quality of executives in British manufacturing needs to be improved along the lines suggested by Continental experience. Such a claim can be justified for what its fulfilment might imply for groups in the community from single mothers dependent on social welfare payments, to pensioners and to harassed politicians. Manufacturing is a major source of national wealth, even in a so-called post-industrial society.

The Continental system teaches us a way of getting a good proportion of the most able members of each generation into manufacturing. Through ideas such as that of *métier* and *Beruf*, and the fact that specialists in particular areas can reach the top, we can see that it is perfectly feasible for someone trained as an engineer or commercial specialist to become the chief executive of his concern. The need is suggested for a coherent system of producing people of this type.

In my other paper, I have made some recommendations for change. We should establish something like the Continental systems of secondary and higher education. For most occupation groups, the rights to set examinations and control entry should be abolished; but they could retain their study and consultative roles, and perhaps engage in collective bargaining. In higher education, new institutions would probably be needed, as the orientation of existing ones towards manufacturing is insubstantial. An emphasis on skill should be made to permeate through the whole system of education, at the expense of emphasis on science.

The most obvious criticism of such an approach concerns the role of the state. On the face of it, what Burrage calls the 'normative' system of the liberal Anglo-Saxon countries, is matched by a Continental-style 'imperative' one. Accusations of 'corporatism' would be heard, along with fears about threats to academic and other forms of individual freedom, if Britain moved towards the Continental way.

There is no reason, however, to believe that such fears need be realised. This is because changes of the type suggested could be designed to fit in quite easily with other changes, some of which are already beginning to occur. Further, there may well exist a great deal of latent demand for several changes of the first kind. Accent on personal skill in work should not be incompatible with increased democracy in education and manufacturing.

The idea of democracy in education suggests that individuals should assimilate information and learn skills that will be useful to them as citizens, and as producers and consumers. A trend towards broader education of the kind suggested would accord with this. With regard to the learning of skills, it is useful to think of Illich's distinction between drills and rituals, and his utopian recommendation that society should be 'deschooled'.

Illich criticises the Western school system, including polytechnics and universities, for its stress on the ideal of the school as a community. Teachers feel morally obliged to use rituals, such as assembly, prayers, and singing the National Anthem, to turn pupils into people who conform to the apparent demands of group living. Yet the skills that pupils want, and need to learn, are essentially personal ones, learned through repeated practice, or drills, as with arithmetical tables. Also work outside the school is very often done by groups put together because they share skills or an interest in producing something.

The school is unable, therefore, to be a microcosm of life outside, and it is skill-averse in this way, as well as in the way in which it tends to emphasise knowledge-specific conceptions of work. Illich also attacks schooling for the false hopes that it engenders of social mobility, through its sought-for political role as an instrument of greater social equality. The Anglo-Saxon professional qualifying associations are 'schools' of a kind, too, through the science-connection, through their stress on responsibility to the community, and their use of highly-sophisticated rituals.

To come back to democracy in education, a democratic system should presumably offer individuals the skills and information that they wish to learn, once the basic job has been done of teaching them ways of learning and what there is to be learned. This is, in fact, what a lot of Continental schooling comes closer to doing than the British kind, through its later specialisation and its much broader and more skill-specific conceptions of vocational education.

This is not to argue that the Continental system is a particularly egalitarian one. It does, however, appear to do a better job, than the British one, at the combination of providing a general education and teaching basic job-specific skills. It also seems much better at setting individuals free to develop their personal skills, partly because there are no professional qualifying associations to muddy the process once full-time education is over.

Finally, it must be emphasised that none of the preceding argument is incompatible with the suggestion that executives in manufacturing should be accountable in some way to their subordinates. Issues of competence and responsibility are partly separate ones, in spite of the claims of professionalism.

References

Barnett C, *The Collapse of British Power*, Methuen, 1972

Burns T, 'Management in action', *Operational Research Quarterly*, Vol 8, 1957

Burrage M, 'Nationalization and the professional ideal', *Sociology*, Vol 7, 1973

Carlson S, *Executive Behaviour: A Study of the Work Load and the Working Methods of Managing Directors*, Strömbergs, Stockholm, 1951

Child J, *British Management Thought: A Critical Analysis*, Unwin, 1969

—'Management', in *The Sociology of Industry* (eds Parker S R, Brown R K, Child J and Smith M A), Unwin, 1972

—and Kieser A, 'The development of organizations over time', University of Aston, 1976

Chisholm A W J, *First Report on the Education and Training of Engineers on the Continent of Europe*, Salford, 1975

Coleman D C, 'Gentlemen and players', *Economic History Review*, Vol 26, 1973

Dubin R, 'Business Behaviour *Behaviourally* Viewed', in *Social Science Approaches to Business Behaviour* (ed G B Strother), Irwin-Dorsey, Homewood, Illinois, 1962

Fores M and Glover I A, 'The real work of executives', *Management Today*, November 1976

—and Glover I A, 'The British disease: professionalism', *The Times Higher Education Supplement*, 24 February 1978

—and Lawrence P and Sorge A, 'Germany's Front-Line Force', *Management Today*, March 1978

Glover I A, 'Executive career patterns: Britain, France, Germany, and Sweden', Paper Eleven in this book

—'Managerial Work: A Review of the Evidence', unpublished literature review, The City University, 1977

Greenwood E, 'Attributes of a profession', *Social Work*, Vol 2, July 1957

Illich I D, *Deschooling Society*, Harper and Row, New York, 1971

Johnson T, 'The Professions in the Class Structure', paper given at the annual conference of the British Sociological Association, March 1975

Kumar K, 'The Salariat', *New Society*, 21 October 1976

Lawrence G, Barham P, Bell G, Jones P, Mant A, and Miller E, *Towards Managerial Development for Tomorrow*, Tavistock, 1975

Mant A, *The Rise and Fall of the British Manager*, Macmillan, 1977

Mintzberg H, *The Nature of Managerial Work,* Harper and Row, New York, 1973

Perkin H, *The Origins of Modern English Society 1780–1880,* Routledge, 1969

Pettigrew A M, *The Politics of Organizational Decision-Making,* Tavistock, 1973

Reader W J, *Professional Men: The Rise of the Professional Classes in Nineteenth-Century England,* Weidenfeld, 1966

Roth J A, 'Professionalism: the sociologist's decoy', *Sociology of Work and Occupations,* Vol 1, February 1974

Sorge A, 'Technical education and training as a public concern in Britain, France and Germany', unpublished paper, Oxford, 1976

Stewart R, *Contrasts in Management,* McGraw-Hill, 1976

Wilensky H L, 'The professionalization of everyone?', *American Journal of Sociology,* Vol 70, September 1964

Knowledge, information and language

Sune Carlson
UNIVERSITY OF UPPSALA, SWEDEN

The author is emeritus professor of business
administration at the University of Uppsala

The scope of this paper is limited to some of the communication problems encountered by top management in manufacturing concerns. The two principle tasks of top management are to administer an organisation, and to represent this organisation towards the outside world. Both these tasks relate to people, or to groups of people. When the chief executive represents his firm to the outside world, he does so to people who represent this outside world. When he administers the organisation, his primary task is to see that necessary decisions are taken and carried out; *ex post* he controls the consequences of these decisions. As administrator he administers the people in the organisation, not its building, machines or stocks of goods. His means of contact with people must necessarily be language.

Decisions are based on opinions and opinions are formed from the existing stock of knowledge, together with new information received from outside. Thus, I use the term knowledge as a stock concept, and the term information as a flow concept. Knowledge is the sum of what we know, and this sum may be increased by information. Both knowledge and information are expressed in language of one kind or another, words, mathematical symbols, chemical formulae, technical drawings, etc. Sums of knowledge and flows of information are a prerequisite of industrial activity.

Stocks of knowledge

Since stocks of knowledge of various kinds are permanently required by the firm, investment in knowledge may be compared with investment in other durable resources, such as plant and equipment. It is generally easy to specify the factory space, the machines and other equipment which the firm possesses or which are required for a particular manufacturing process: but it is very hard to define the knowledge which is needed for the same process, or the total knowledge which the firm has at its disposal. One of the reasons for this difficulty is that, to a large extent, knowledge is stored in people's minds. New knowledge is often obtained by the employment of someone who is believed to possess this knowledge. A firm may perhaps be able to make some kind of inventory of the knowledge which is stored in reports, manuals, drawings and other records; but to make an inventory of what exists in people's minds is impossible. An outside observer may note a certain lack of knowledge in a firm, just as a professor may observe a certain lack of knowledge in a student; but the professor can never find out everything the student really knows and no-one can ever record the total knowledge which the firm has at its disposal.

'Knowledge is power' was a common slogan in the Swedish socialist papers when I was a young man. But knowledge is power, only if we can prevent other people from gaining access to it. It is secret knowledge which gives monopoly power, yet it is difficult to prevent knowledge from leaking out and other people from using it.

Here we have another difference between investment in knowledge and investment in other durable resources.

It is obvious that a worker who leaves his employment must not use tools which belong to the old company on his new job. But what part of the knowledge which a sub-contractor or a sales engineer has picked up from a particular company may he, or may he not, use freely? That is hard to say. Since it is difficult to draw a boundary between company secrets and freely available knowledge, most firms try to play safe by keeping a lot of knowledge secret, which in reality is available to anybody who is willing to make an effort to get it.

There is one important exception to all this. By taking out special patents or copyrights, the owner of a patent or a design may get the exclusive right to use these; and he can forbid unauthorised use, though only for a certain time. He gets a temporary monopoly of a certain body of knowledge based on the law, in exchange for a monopoly based on secrecy.

The existence of patent rights and copyrights makes it possible to transfer knowledge protected by such rights to others by licensing agreements. But the trade in patents and copyrights is a much more complicated affair than trade in other durable resources. Even more complicated, however, is the transfer of knowledge which is not protected by patents or copyrights. This is done by means of what are called know-how agreements. Since it is difficult to specify exactly the knowledge which the agreement covers, how it must be used, and what the use of this knowledge is worth, many firms are reluctant to sign such agreements.

Another difference between investment in knowledge and investment in other durable resources concerns depreciation and obsolescence. While plant and equipment depreciate by being used, knowledge does not. On the contrary, the use of knowledge gives rise to additional knowledge, by which the total stock is increased. But because we live in a changing world, knowledge may become obsolete; the faster the development is, the quicker knowledge is disseminated, and the more specific the knowledge is, the higher the rate of obsolescence becomes.

All this leads to investment in knowledge generally being regarded in accounting practice as a rather dubious asset, of questionable value as security for loans. The payments are generally written off quickly for knowledge purchased from outside the firm in the form of patent rights or 'goodwill' payments in connection with mergers; and the cost of new knowledge produced inside the firm is written off at once. From a theoretical point of view it is, of course, the discounted future income from an investment which determines its value, irrespective of whether the investment is made in knowledge or in material resources. In practice, the two types of investment are evaluated differently, not only by the firm's banker but by the management itself.

Information and language

As mentioned above, decisions are based on opinions, and opinions are formed on the basis of the stock of knowledge already existing and new information received. Also the control activity is almost entirely based on incoming information. A characteristic feature of top management's working experience is that its members rarely get any information directly by observation of facts or events on the spot, such as during inspection tours of plants and warehouses. Most information, instead, comes from people, some in the form of records and memos, some as oral reports, or by *ad hoc* statements in conversation, or in committee meetings. The larger the organisation is, the more important written communication becomes.

Before a communication reaches the top executive a whole series of activities has already taken place:
(a) First there are observations of things and events to be made, and from these observations relevant data have to be recorded. The language used for this recording is often highly specialised and understood only by the technicians in the particular field.
(b) In most cases these recordings have to be encoded into signals, transmitted through communication and data processing channels and decoded back again. These latter activities, which have their own technical language, are the subject of study in so-called information theory. But they need not concern us here so much.
(c) When the data are received at the executive level of the firm, or the staff levels next to the executive level, they have to be evaluated, as regards validity. They are then interpreted, as to their relevance for decisions which have to be made. They also have to be transformed into documentation and language suitable to the particular decision

maker and decision situation. The more the decision maker is familiar with the technical language originally used, and the general conditions at the data collection stage, the easier this transformation will be. A former research and development man will, for example, require a different kind of accounting report from a former finance man.

It is interesting to note that while we know a great deal, and there exists a vast literature, about the data collection and data transmission parts of information flows, we know relatively little about aspects of evaluation and interpretation. But one thing seems certain. The larger the stock of knowledge which the firm already possesses in a particular field, the easier and the cheaper it will be to get additional information. A firm with a well educated technical staff has an advantage in matters of evaluation and interpretation of technical data, and in most cases it has better connections than other firms with research institutions and professional associations.

Part of the data needed by top management is collected inside the firm. Another part is collected from outside by the firm's own staff. But by far the most part of the information needed consists of external data supplied by an outside agent. Because of economies of scale and specialisation, and because of his geographical proximity to the original source of information, such an agent can often collect data more cheaply than the firm itself. He may also combine the collection of information with other activities, and save costs in that way. For example, a bank must collect data on the credit-worthiness of its clients in connection with its regular lending activities; if the firm in question needs some additional information of this type, it can easily be supplied. But when the firm needs unusual and very specific information, such as complicated technical details about products or processes, there may be little or no savings in using an outside agency.

An agent can lower his own costs of collecting data and his charges to clients, if he can distribute the same information to several clients at the same time. But since different clients generally have somewhat different information needs, this can be done only by increasing the number of items in every information package. For the recipient firm this means that it gets more information than it wants. Some of the data may be of no relevance to the decision requirements, and they may be expressed in a technical jargon hard to understand. That is, instead of specifically needed information, the firm gets general information, from which it must pick out the particular items it needs. Thus, the collection costs for the information have gone down, but interpretation costs have increased. The uniqueness and complexity of the information needed determine how much more expensive it becomes to interpret data collected and put together by an outsider. It may be quite easy, for example, to pick out and evaluate the relevant data from a trade paper on the general price and payment developments in a certain country. It is much more difficult to select the relevant parts of a scientific report on complicated technical processes and to evaluate these data. The costs of interpreting such information depend, of course, very much on the stock of knowledge the firm already has.

The irrationale of information

Thus far in this paper, the analysis has been based on certain assumptions which have not been clearly stated but have, I hope, been understood. It has been assumed that the top management:
(a) knows what information it needs for decision and control purposes;
(b) that it determines itself what information it wants to get;
(c) that it knows where to get it; and
(d) when information has been received, the top management knows what to do with it. That is to say, the top executive knows how to make up his mind.

But in reality life is not that simple.

In making a decision, the management of the firm is faced with a series of alternative possibilities, on which it has formed certain opinions. The chosen set of alternatives which are considered in the final selection process may be regarded as a sub-set of a larger set of possible alternatives, which the management has reviewed only superficially and which it has some opinion about; knowledge of the larger set is not as reliable as that of the chosen set.

The larger set may, in its turn, be regarded as a sub-set of a still larger universal set of alternatives, about which the management knows even less or nothing at all. The management cannot directly miss something, or ask for something, of which it does not know the existence. It understands, of course, that there must exist a lot of unknown information that may be relevant to a decision, now or in the future, but it does not know what information this comprises. The same holds true for the control function. You cannot control everything, and possibly what you are actually controlling is not exactly the right thing.

Since the management of a firm seldom knows exactly what information it wants, when it buys information from outside, it pays for an option to draw on a more or less defined stock of knowledge, rather than for specific information. A good example is know-how agreements.

They generally contain an option enabling the buyer to get information on anything the seller knows in a defined area, and it is this option that costs money. In addition the buyer usually pays a variable charge, which covers the seller's direct costs for the reproduction of drawings, manuals and other information material. The membership fees paid to research and trade associations, and the retainer fees paid to consultants, are also, in reality, payments for options to draw on certain stocks of knowledge, rather than payments for specific information flows.

Several studies indicate that top executives rely, in their decision making function, to a large extent on human contacts for their information. This is particularly true of events and circumstances outside the firm. When the executive attends meetings and lunches with representatives of official authorities, trade associations, scientific institutions and company boards, and when he travels abroad, he picks up a lot of information which he uses in his job. But what he picks up is to a large extent determined by other people. It is seldom the result of any conscious search. The same is pretty well true of the information he gets from human contacts inside his firm.

As a consequence of the time the top executive has to spend in formal meetings and outside the firm, his face-to-face contacts with some of his colleagues and subordinates may become very limited without his desiring it, or even noticing it. Entry to his office may become the exclusive preserve of aggressive types of people, or of those who have their offices close to his own. As a result of this, the flow of information reaching him becomes biased with too much emphasis on things which can be measured and reported in statistical tables, and too little emphasis on qualitative and personal comments. The information he gets is, of course, also influenced by the top executive's own occupational background, his personal interests, his likes and dislikes.

Again we come across the question of language. The top executive gets, first of all, the things that people know that he wants to have; his subordinates are all only human beings to act in this way. One of the main findings of a study of executive work, which I made long ago, was that the influence of office layouts was very strong on the communication patterns. This observation has been verified again and again in later research.

Previously I pointed out that the information which the top executive gets from human contact is seldom the result of conscious search. This often stems from the fact that the top executive does not know where to search. He generally meets people of the same age, the same background and the same social standing as himself; and these people are not necessarily the best informed. To establish close contacts with people of another age-group, or of another social group, is not so easy, even if one wants to do so. An executive in a large Swedish organisation confessed to me once that, when he was younger and before he became technical director of his organisation, he knew all the bright young research fellows at the Royal Technical Institute in Stockholm; through them he could keep himself well informed about what was going on in his own specialised field. Today, when he goes there, he is met with a combination of deep respect and suspicion, which does not produce the same type of information he used to get.

Finally, and in reality, most top executives do not form their opinions on information, as it was assumed earlier, but on other people's opinions. They need help to make up their minds. What they have to evaluate is not merely the trustworthiness and usefulness of information, but also the trustworthiness and usefulness of opinions. In business management, the knowledge on which decisions are based, as Frank Knight has so neatly put it, 'is not knowledge of situations and problems and of means of effecting changes, but is knowledge of other men's knowledge of these things'.

A proper use of science

Michael Fores
DEPARTMENT OF INDUSTRY

The author is a senior economic adviser at the
Department of Industry. The views expressed are
personal

It is clear that someone used to dealing with knowledge and information in the systematic way which is associated with science is likely to be a useful person to have in executive posts in manufacturing concerns: such knowledge is always in demand in any enterprise. Yet, it is equally clear that someone whose main working experience is in deriving systematic knowledge, in the scientific tradition, is unlikely to be the right person for executive jobs: the personal skills used vary considerably between business and scholarship.

Executive work, especially towards the top of concerns invariably deals with a complex set of variables, many of which cannot be measured, and for some of which little is known. Even for a simple machine in a factory, those who run things will know how it works; they can normally fix it, when it goes wrong, or have it fixed: but they do not know why it works in the full sense of the optimism of scientific inquiry. The same goes for systems which include people.

Indeed it is fair to say that the business executive inhabits a world much of which is unknowable as well as being unknown. Despite this, however, evidence shows that those running large concerns in manufacturing in successful countries as different as the USA, France, Japan and Germany are likely to have the sort of university-level diploma which indicates a good introduction to the mysteries of one or another branch of science. The chief executive of one very large French concern has three such diplomas.

The basic argument against putting too much emphasis on science in executive work in manufacturing, besides the one about an unknowable world, stems from the fact that the scientist, in deriving knowledge, will normally control variables in a way which is rarely open to the executive. Indeed, by this token, neither of the two most distinctive features of much of scientific inquiry – continuous and disinterested observation of events, and controlled experiment – is readily available to the executive in his place of work. Often there simply is not the time, even if there is the inclination, to observe and record observations with accuracy. Whereas controlled experiment is notoriously difficult to set up in the sorts of social environment in which the executive finds himself to be operating in the process of manufacture.

In an article on what executive work really seems to be in practice, Glover and I argued that there are three particular and separate ways in which science and such work may be connected; yet each strand of connection is looser than many people imagine and looser than the textbooks imply. We also argued, as he has put it in his paper in this book, that the compilation of management science was as much to do with giving status to executives, as with providing a widely-useful body of knowledge.

First, executive work is certainly not scientific when outputs are considered. In manufacturing, the unit's main output takes the form of a bulky artifact; whereas the main output of the scientific process always takes the form of knowledge. Second, most business executives' lives are so unpredictable, and so fractured between planned and actual use of time, that it is difficult, though not impossible, to study their work in an accepted scientific manner. The typical manager is not the reflective type of planner of the textbook stereotype; in reality he is much more often a fixer: a mobile character, carrying with him the firefighter's axe as well as the doctor's healing hand. Third, the gap between executive activity and science is wider than many imagine, because the techniques of management science are not used consistently and successfully.

It is tempting to draw an analogy here between typical executive work and work in engineering. A specially-English phrase 'applied science' implies that the engineer at work is close to the physicist or the chemist. In reality he rarely is, since much of his effort has completely different aims from those of the natural scientist.

Personal flair

Up to this point, the flavour of this paper may be thought to be 'anti-science' in some way. Certainly, my remarks indicate acceptance of the prime importance of some sort of managerial 'flair' which is needed in higher jobs in manufacturing concerns. Yet science is simply a type of knowledge, nothing else. It is knowledge which has gone some way down the road towards being tested for its truth. Only a fool would be against the use of such knowledge. Yet, equally, only a fool will use something which is presented to him under the banner of its being 'scientific', if it proves not to be an aid to his work.

We have been excessively badly served, in the English language, by popular ideas of science and art, and so too of knowledge and skill. In the following section, I plan to deal with other ideas of science from that put forward in the previous paragraph. Here, in dealing with the role of personal skill, or 'flair', in executive work in manufacturing, I quote an argument from Jay, and choose two cases from areas of activity far away from manufacturing.

Jay thinks that the idea of management is 'insulting and belittling', as it implies that the executive is simply put in to mind the shop. There is an implication that the manager simply does what he is told, whereas creative work is done by 'long-haired, clever and irresponsible' people. Jay thinks that leadership is becoming more and more concerned with change', and this is obviously to do with creativity. 'A leader may change the map of Europe, or the breakfast habits of a nation, or the capital structure of an engineering corporation: but changing things is central to leadership, and changing them before anyone else is creativeness.'

On a special type of successful leadership, one of Nelson's biographers, Warner, talks of his form of control of subordinates as 'ordered liberty', a method unusual for the time. Like Marlborough before him, Nelson seems to have been quite happy for his opponents to know what his plan of battle would be. He relied instead, for winning, on a high level of technical and detailed competence in the fleet and on the 'Nelson touch', a kind of special personal flair of his own to weld it all together.

'I believe my arrival was most welcome', wrote Nelson to Lady Hamilton three weeks before Trafalgar, with a confident lack of modesty, which Britons would shy away from using to-day, 'not only to the Commander but also to every individual in it, and when I came to explain the "Nelson touch" it was like an electric shock. Some shed tears, all approved – "It was new – it was singular – it was simple" and from Admirals downwards, it was repeated–"It must succeed, if ever they will allow us to get at them!" '

Now Warner's summary:

'The cult of Nelson has continued, and it has swollen into an industry almost as ramified as that of Shakespeare. A century after Trafalgar, learned commentators set to work to analyse the battle, perhaps in the hope of unravelling the secret of Nelson's tactics. They could have spared their pains, for the pith of the matter lay in Nelson's ability to seize whatever opportunities came his way, without regard to rules, precedents or tradition, and to squeeze the last ounce out of what was offered.'

This comment is apt about a man who was reputed to have turned his telescope to his blind eye to avoid following his superior's foolish orders at the Battle of Copenhagen. I will return later to learned commentators and introduce the idea that the scribbler may often be jealous of those of his subjects who are rather more dashing than he.

A second quotation is nearer to us in time, but just as far from manufacturing in type of product deriving from work. The accent, as in the case of the assessment of Nelson's effectiveness, is on personal skills. In the *Daily Mail*, this theme was taken up by James on our soccer, 'the oak that grew up twisted'. The base of our football is 750 000

schoolboys playing weekly; yet the national team could not beat
Finnish part-timers emphatically. The reason for this is:

'because the men who tended the acorns misunderstood their task. We have bred an
entire generation of footballers who can fight, survive, endure . . . but who have forgotten,
if they ever learned, how to play. Obsessed with making our game "competitive" we have
lost the notion that a footballer's first task is to establish a mastery not over other men
but over the ball itself.

'It all began 20 years ago when coaching became the new science, or religion . . . .
Teaching team patterns to people who could already play was one thing . . . but Hackney
Marshes Winterbottoms were ramming "method" down the throats of kids who a week
earlier had innocently thought of this greatest game as still a game.

'Suddenly there were new dimensions for kids who wanted merely to dribble. They were
re-classified "sweepers". Boys who had taken overwhelming delight in being able to shoot
were bemused by instructions on how to "mark space".

'Worse, there was suddenly no place for the individual, little mercy for the mischievous
mind, none for the meagre in build. For winning was what it was all about . . . and team
places went to the big, the strong and, especially, the obedient.

'Thus the game at this level of learning was taken over by schoolmasters who wanted to
walk tall in the staffroom; scoutmasters who picked up the jargon from Jimmy Hill and
went away to burden their charges with leaden lumps of theory; youth leaders who seized
on notions like "work rate" as the panacea to their position in some obscure league.'

A snap comparison between England's unsuccessful football team
and Nelson's victorious fleet is not so inappropriate for the theme of
this paper. At Trafalgar and before, it seems clear that each English
ship, and those in them, were more proficient than their adversaries
in the details of the arts of navigation, seamanship and gunnery. The
whole mixture was very successfully put together with the daring
and quick-thinking brio of their admiral. A football team of eleven
men depends more than a fleet on the special personal qualities of each
individual, as the sad English display for the World Cup will have
shown. When the captain gets so heavily engaged himself, as the
footballer-captain, he has less chance to exercise the leadership of a
Nelson. A fleet can have weak links; and one sailor can fill in for
another when the first is killed, injured, loses heart or goes mad. In
contrast members of a football team must, in some measure, be all
chiefs and no Indians. Something more than graft, teamwork,
cohesion and method is needed. Perhaps it is the mysterious 'flair'
again, quality X, a kind of personal magic which can penetrate where
reason does not go.

After all, the justification for action in fields as diverse as battle,
football and executive work in manufacturing is success; in face of this,
the scientist's yardsticks of reason and truth only get a modest look-in.
As criteria, they are part of the rules of another game. Another *Mail*
writer summed up the 1976 Italy–England match in Rome harping at

quality X: 'in the end it came down to a question of inspiration. In that less tangible quality, Italy were unchallenged'. I suspect that success in manufacturing is about the same sort of thing.

What is science?

I suggested earlier that there is no doubt what science is. Probably not all would agree with the definition used. However, after examining other conceptions of science at some length, there is no way to go except to the primary one, which makes it the same as the German *Wissenschaft*, all knowledge. Other conceptions simply do not work.

'Science', for instance, as one side of a 'two cultures' gap breaks down very quickly as a useful and consistent idea. Some commentators, amongst them Snow, have classed engineering and 'technology' as part of the 'science' side of the gap, perhaps because engineers learn physics at college. The criterion for classing people together in these terms is that 'without thinking about it, they (members of a cultural group) respond alike. That is what a culture means'.

But evidence suggests that the engineer and the natural scientist do not act and respond alike: one is concerned with making things and the other with observing things. And it takes little imagination to see that the whole cultural-gap conception was no more than a veiled attempt to argue that the man from the lab should be more in evidence in decision-making. Indeed, one of the cleverest natural scientists of this century, Bernal, so twisted an interpretation of history to fit the unsuitable 'applied science' model, that he put the caveman with his sticks and stones at the start of his classic study of science in society. Furthermore, 'science policy', spawned by the Bernalite–Cambridge tradition turns out bizarrely to be as much to do with manufacture as with science itself.

Despite Snow's now-famous Rede lecture, man away from Oxbridge high tables has always managed to reconcile any potentially-conflicting requirements of science and art, of knowledge and skill, at work or elsewhere. As for manufacturing, empirical study shows that even the most discontinuous types of technical change, known as innovations, do not typically stem from a new use of the knowledge of science. Instead the importance of scientific knowledge flows into manufacturing from its ambient nature. It can as well find a use in cooking, police work or sculpting, as in work on product, process or system improvement.

Another idea of science is essentially tautologous, though common none-the-less. We are accustomed to hearing about branches of knowledge or areas of teaching as 'disciplines', or as separate 'sciences'. Use of either term tends to give distinction to a subject-area. But, in fact, what has normally happened is that all the 'scientists' have come to an agreement about mutual borders; that is all. Such agreement can incorporate some very partial judgement, as I will aim to show subsequently.

As an example of this second idea of science, Robbins wrote a classic study called *An Essay on the Nature and Significance of Economic Science*. The most significant fact that the reader derives from this essay is that Robbins has a horror that economics might be too much associated with history. The latter subject is to do with particular interpretation, in his view; whereas economics aims towards the general. In my usage, of course, history is as much a science as physics. To argue that physics is distinctive by being an 'exact science' is to forget Heisenberg and Einstein; in all branches of science you can only approach the truth, but never reach it. Yet, more significant for the theme of this paper, Robbins never managed to arrive at a basic and explicit meaning of his own topic. 'Economic science', to him, is simply what is taught by economists, with all the suppressed border disputes thrown in. This includes, of course, no real definition of what a science is, except a nursemaidly assertion that 'a science is what I say it is'.

A third meaning of science, one which would not be worth bothering with if this paper and conference were not to do with management, is implied by the quotation below. Dale and Michelon argue, in *Modern Management Methods*, on the 'job of management':

'Management is not an exact science like physics and chemistry. Although many things have been discovered about it, it is essential that the manager use judgement, based on good sense and experience. And this is not a bad thing. For if he could manage by merely following a set of rules, the management job would be far less interesting than it is.'

I have already argued that physics and chemistry, despite their access to controlled experiment in the lab, are not 'exact sciences'. The intended distinction between 'exact' and 'inexact' in science is virtually meaningless and normally confusing even to those who aim to act upon it: all branches of science are inexact. Furthermore, the use of 'judgement' by practitioners of any sort does not prevent their activity from being a part of the scientific process: physicists and chemists use judgement, common sense, experience and flair in their aim to write down knowledge of natural events. Finally, it is quite ridiculous to bring up a moralistic point in the context of deciding whether a process is part of science or not. Microbiology could be as monotonous or as challenging, to one or to all, without its making the slightest difference to its being a science. And, besides that, if Einstein had followed 'a set of rules' given to him, we might never have learnt about relativity.

These comments should be sufficient to show that Dale and his collaborator were ploughing an arid furrow, in their skirmish with 'science'. A later comment that 'the basic management function is planning' implies that they were telling fairy stories about executives at work. Carlson's pioneering study, published 15 years before *Modern Management Methods*, had already nailed that lie. Yet the essential point to make is one put forward earlier. Neither management, nor any other activity, can sensibly be thought of as a science (with science here described as a process), unless the activity produces a main output of knowledge put out for test. And management in manufacturing certainly does not produce such a primary output.

Creativity

In the section of this paper which follows the present one, I discuss a model of knowledge transfer which aims to show some elements of a proper use of science for those outside the laboratory. Here, the argument returns briefly to the first obsession with 'flair' and personal skill, ideas which include both the 'Nelson touch' and the ability to make the ball do what you want in soccer.

There is something rather odd in our culture which allows Jay to be able to assert, quite rightly in my view, that creativity is normally thought to be the preserve of the unwashed Bohemian rather than the man in the street. In the same passage, he singles out his surprise when, fresh from the world of TV, which is always discussing the subject, he found creativity in an unassuming engineering factory . . . 'after a a week or two it suddenly dawned on me that a television programme and an engineering product went through a virtually identical process and demanded almost exactly the same qualities from the people responsible for them'.

Of course, there are many who could have told Jay something of this sort years before. Yet my point is that they did not; or at least the message had not got through. There is a high-brow world in our British conception, which incidentally includes both 'cultural' groupings of Snow's Cambridge high table. In this world, true creativity is thought to belong to 'us', and not to the 'them' of manufacturing where preoccupations are held to be humdrum and without major challenge.

I do not aim to argue that it is nobler, more challenging, or even more useful to change the breakfast habits of a nation, or to make an improved sludge-cock, than to change the face of Europe (following Jay's passage). Yet man is distinctively and perennially creative. This happens usually over the long haul, rather than in the short dramatic bursts beloved of many commentators on the subject. Most people in higher posts in all walks of life are paid for their creativity. In our culture, it should be better accepted that flair and creativity are as much in demand in manufacturing as they are in the fine arts or natural science.

To illustrate this last point, it is well known that, in the second half of the eighteenth century, something was stirring in the workshop. In the preface to a study of *The Western Intellectual Tradition*, Bronowski and Mazlish, following the Bernalite–Cambridge tradition, stressed a view that 'the steam engine helped to shape the modern world at least as much as Napoleon and Adam Smith', and that this fact showed the importance of 'science'. Yet even a handbook of the 'Science Museum' argues that this invention had little to do with the new use of scientific knowledge. Instead of science, of course, it was personal skill and creativity which produced the steam engine. Yet, Bronowski and his co-author seem to have been reluctant to accept that such qualities exist in manufacturing.

The House of Science: a model

A knowledge-transfer model is used to amplify themes introduced earlier, more in a definitional than an operational way. The model concerns the habits of two central characters, the activist and the observer; and of one less central character, the professional.

The activist goes in search of knowledge, and to obtain this he enters the House of Science. This is a round house, dimly-lit, hushed and built rather like the apse of a medieval cathedral, but without the altar as the centre of the circle which forms the apse. There are fifty to a hundred separate chapels in the House of Science, each clustering around the circumference of the building. Each chapel is guarded by a door; and scientists are at work behind each one of them observing as best they might with the apparatus they have. These scientists are the observers of the model.

If the activist, who may be a manufacturer, wants knowledge from observers, he has to come to the House of Science and shop around. An advantage about scientific knowledge is that it is a free good;

no price is paid on transfer. However, as the scientist does not benefit financially when his findings are useful, he has little impetus to open up the chapel door. The activist's search for knowledge is made more difficult in this way, for the observer aims his findings primarily at his group of peers; these are the people who will test them for their contribution to science itself.

A third person in the model is the professional who gives advice to the activist from a particular book of science. The activist comes to the centre of the circle made by the House of Science. The only person to try his hand at giving advice to him directly is the professional, a sort of go-between whose principal stated role is that he will help the activist avoid the bother of knocking at the chapel doors himself. Of course, if this process is successful, it will save time; but it will also cost money.

For the activist, life at the centre of the House of Science is rather lonely; he is like a townsman visiting the country. Unless he knows the ropes and is familiar with the ways of science, he will experience a very windswept feeling. Should he turn this way or that, because of the persuasion of particular professionals, intermediaries who can go some way to speaking his language and understanding his preoccupations? Or should he go where no professionals offer their services, and so knock on particular doors himself? In the latter case, he can find out exactly what the observers can offer and how they describe what they are doing.

One lesson which is clear to me from the operation of this model is that the activist who knows what life is like in one of the chapels of science is at a great advantage over another who has not had this firsthand experience. Not that familiarity necessarily breeds contempt, or even enthusiasm. However it can breed instead the kind of scepticism which will make it more likely that the scientifically-trained activist will not readily be hood-winked by the mysteries of a particular science and by the special pleading which the specialist can often put forward. Quite simply as well, such an activist will know how to frame his questions and may have a hunch about the form of reply to expect.

In this context, the differing aims of the activist and the observer must be made clear. Essentially the first is keen to produce particular solutions (artifacts or systems), using any knowledge available from any branch of science; whereas the second strives for general solutions (statements or hypotheses) using particularly the knowledge which has become available in his own chapel. With such differing basic aims, life-styles vary greatly between members of the two groups. The activist finds it difficult to think and react like the observer. Perhaps more important, the onus is definitely on the first to accommodate to the second, as the activist wants the knowledge transfer, rather than the observer who is invariably more interested in getting his findings accepted by his peer group of scientists.

To catch the spirit of the activist's life-style, most of the maverick writers on management and organization seem to me to do a better job than the majority of the sober battalion, even sober commentators whose work is widely read and recommended. Heller on *The Naked Manager*, Townsend's *Up the Organization*, Peter and his principle, *How to Succeed in Business Without Really Trying*, even C Northcote Parkinson, who is not distinctive as a writer on business and commerce, are all capable of picturing the activist's world. Yet this is not the whole story, especially if my model of the House of Science tells a tale which has any use.

Probably the most important points to be made from the model are that:
(a) the activist must borrow directly from science in a selective fashion: he certainly does not buy;
(b) he should be wary of professional advisers, unless he keeps them 'in house', in his own unit, and/or understands their degree of competence; their interpretations may be biased;
(c) the activist's aims, activities and way of life are quite different from the observer's.

The breakdown of science

The argument now picks up a point made earlier, but not drawn out centrally in the model. I noted the horror which comes out in many passages of Robbins' book on economics, that someone might confuse the subject with history. This is a boundary horror. The point was also made that the classification of parts of the totality of science, *Wissenschaft*, all knowledge, has always been arbitrary. So the name on the door of any of the chapels round the scientific apse can be arbitrary, dependent on the strength of bargaining power of different groups at the time when border disputes were solved.

An example of how this process takes place can be seen briefly from a study of Anglo-Saxon archaeology. At the end of the last century, according to one commentator, archaeology came from antiquarianism to 'a rigid discipline based on two methods of study – excavation and typology': it also became a science and so became respectable. 'By collaboration', argues the same author 'the archaeologist and historian

can enlarge each others' experience . . .'. But surely, as the intelligent
layman might think to himself, archaeology is in fact a part of history,
rather than being contrasted with history; it is this simply because it
deals with the past. However this point is neglected in an academic
breakdown which agrees demarcations within the whole body of
science, knowledge and scholarship. A quiet voice has uttered. Traditionally the historian deals with documentary evidence, whereas the
archaeologist deals with solid remains, many of them in the form of
artifacts. So, this is how it must always be!

The name on the door of a scientific chapel may be arbitrary; so is
the spread of inquiry inside. Physics deals with matter; and so, oddly,
does chemistry. Whereas the matter which is part of living organisms is
the subject of biology; or is it the subject of organic chemistry?
Sociology is the study of man in groups; whereas psychology is the
study of man himself. However, individuals form groups; so some of
social behaviour is part of individual behaviour. And anthropology,
with its accent on culture, also deals with man in groups. But so does
economics, and a part of history. As social science cannot normally
conduct controlled experiment, is each of its branches constrained to
produce findings which are only partial, or at least only a partial
explanation of events?

What, more centrally for this paper, is the proper part of science to
turn to for those executives in manufacturing industry who have to deal
with people and matter concurrently, with 'socio-technical systems' in a
phrase which sounds good but often gives little extra understanding for
what has to be done? We have biochemistry, physical chemistry,
biophysics, social psychology. Should there be a door in the House of
Science called socio-chemistry or anthro-physics or eco-zoology (the
animal aspects of wider housekeeping)? I think not; but posing the
question outlines the activist's dilemma. As argued beforehand, the
executive will have to shop around, whatever the names on the doors of
the chapels around the apse of the House of Science. Each factory is a
culture; so anthropology may even help. Someone called a 'manager'
will not find all he needs behind the label 'management science'. A
knowledge of psychology or materials science may be crucial in production, geography or history in marketing. And so on.

A socio-manufacturing system: the importance of detail

One important strand in the subject of the best use of science in
manufacturing has been left to the end of this paper, because of its

importance rather than a lack of it. However much scientific knowledge and scientific method are used in executive work, this type of work is inevitably more concerned with detail than with principle. So, it contrasts with the world of the scientist, if only because the scientist aims to test and put forward principles as his major working contribution.

We are used to talk about systems; and I referred earlier to the idea of a socio-technical system. To draw attention to my point, I coin the phrase 'socio-manufacturing system' for the lump of reality which an executive in a manufacturing concern has to deal with. The social part of this system is more familiar to most audiences, since most have read a little sociology; whereas the process of making artifacts outside the garden shed is far less well known to most.

Much of the process of manufacturing is best thought of, to outsiders, as turning science on its head. The scientist observes, classifies and aims for general statements, put out for test about their truth, and expressed in words and symbols on paper. Of course, the manufacturer has to observe his process and classify in a way which ensures that everyone agrees what a sludgecock is. But his proper preoccupation is with a particular solution, rather than a general application; and truth is never his output. Indeed, in the unknowable and unknown world referred to before, anyone who finds himself obsessed with a search for the truth is something of a fool. And, as Derek de Solla Price has argued in a classic exposition, attitudes to paper vary. To the manufacturer, a paper on what he has done is simply icing on the cake. To almost all in the academy it is the way that their competence is judged.

The stark contrast in modes of work is perhaps best summed up in this remark; the natural scientist aims to break up the material world into its component parts to understand its composition. The manufacturer aims to put the material world together in a different configuration from that found naturally.

I return to one point made earlier, in the context of the importance of detail in a socio-manufacturing system. The scholar and the writer are sometimes jealous of the activist; the remark quoted from Warner on Nelson points to this. 'Learned commentators' have wanted to believe that Nelson's success depended in a substantial way on a plan, or perhaps a 'science', rather than on the 'Nelson touch'. And 'learned commentators' are those who have built up the book of science, which stresses the importance of principle.

The lack of good communication between scientist and manufacturer stems from a different feeling for detail in very different worlds. Of course, a concern for detail is important in scientific inquiry. The detail of observational data is crucial to get right; and the researcher becomes obsessed with his subject-matter. Yet the picture of science which most people carry around with them is one of a hierarchical structure, which results from the aim to derive laws or principles which are ever more generally applicable.

By and large, for a manufacturer, principle of this type is relatively unimportant. As an example, machines are constantly being constructed in a regime in which not only are relationships not understood, but some of the general assumptions are incorrect. This is the unknowable world mentioned before, in which even basic items such as Newton's law of motion are inexact. To the manufacturer the type of detail which is his obsession is typically artifact-detail or market-detail. Components have to be right to fit together and work properly in an object which will sell. To the constructor, for example, what is known about the nature of a material is normally taken as given; whereas he is most concerned about getting component P to fit component Q, using machine R, operator S and executive T, all below a certain cost, to get to the market U by time V with each of P–V being adaptable, changeable or negotiable. The game is a different one from that of science, each with its own set of challenges. The differences must be well understood by those in manufacturing who wish to make a proper use of science.

References

Bernal J D, *Science in History*, Watts, 1954

Bronowski J and Mazlish B, *The Western Intellectual Tradition*, Hutchinson, 1960

Carlson S, *Executive Behaviour*, Strömbergs, Stockholm, 1951

Dale E and Michelon L C, *Modern Management Methods*, World Publishing, 1966

Fores M, 'Snow, universities and the generalist', *Higher Education Review*, Spring 1971

—'Science policy: a misleading enigma', unpublished paper, 1977

—'Science of science: a substantial fraud', *Higher Education Review*, Summer 1977

—and Glover I, 'The real work of executives', *Management Today*, November 1976

—Lawrence P and Sorge A, 'Germany's Front-Line Force', *Management Today* March 1978

Glover I, 'Executive career patterns: Britain, France, Germany and Sweden', Paper Eleven in this book

—'Professionalism and manufacturing industry', Paper Eight in this book.

Hudson L, 'Prime movers', paper for Department of Industry, 1975

James B, 'The oak that grew up twisted', *Daily Mail*, 15 October 1976

Jay A, *Management and Machiavelli*, Hodder, 1967

Price D de S, 'Is technology historically independent of science?', *Technology and Culture*, Fall 1965

Robbins L, *An Essay on the Nature and Significance of Economic Science*, Macmillan, 1935

Snow C P, *The Two Cultures and The Scientific Revolution*, CUP, 1959

Warner O, *Nelson*, Weidenfeld, 1975

Wilson D, *The Anglo-Saxons*, Penguin, 1971

Executive career patterns: Britain, France, Germany and Sweden

Ian Glover
THE CITY UNIVERSITY

The author is on the academic research staff at The City University.
This paper was originally published in *Energy World* in
December 1976, since when a number of amendments
have been made

In France, Germany and Sweden, between 80 and 90 per cent of the top executives in large firms are graduates, whereas the equivalent British figure is about 50 per cent. Although many of Britain's top executives who are not graduates do have professional qualifications, generally obtained by part-time study, the executive cadres of the other three countries also include many individuals with vocational qualifications of a roughly equivalent standard, while they are generally more highly qualified. One very important feature of the British–Continental comparison is the relatively poor representation of men with technical backgrounds at top level in British firms.

Lack of investment in manufacturing has probably been the most popular of the conventional reasons offered in recent years for the industrial part of Britain's economic problem. However, studies of the relationships between levels of investment and productivity in different industries, and in different countries, indicate that the truth lies elsewhere and is more complicated.

Other industrial countries have invested no more in manufacturing as a proportion of output, but have had higher rates of growth. Also, detailed evidence about firms and industries shows that there is no simple relationship between investment and growth. Moreover, international comparison shows that Britain's real weakness lies in her inability to secure a good rate of return on her existing capital. The argument that sees lack of investment mainly as an important symptom, rather than as the main cause, of the unsatisfactory performance of Britain's manufacturing sector is becoming increasingly popular. What else, therefore, may have caused our decline?

Evidence concerning the quality of Britain's top executive cadres, comparing them with their counterparts in three countries which have been economically more successful since 1945, suggests a great deal about the situation. So to understand Britain's use of her manpower may prove more fruitful than to exhibit a concern that focuses on investment. The comparisons involved are much more striking than is the case with investment. More significantly, commonsense indicates that a country's ability to train and deploy its people intelligently is the most fundamental determinant of its ability to use the physical resources at its command. The countries that are the most successful at training a good proportion of the most able members of each generation for jobs that produce wealth, are likely to be those that are consistently successful in producing wealth. Conversely, those countries whose institutions work to discourage such people from entering wealth-creating employment, and who fail to train those who do in a very effective fashion, are not likely to fare as well.

The evidence presented here about the educational, professional and occupational, and social backgrounds of British executives in industry suggests that the UK falls into the second of these two categories. Evidence on managerial backgrounds in France, Germany and Sweden suggests that all these countries fall into the first, in spite of their different industrial and political histories.

Significantly, these countries have different attitudes towards occupations, to the use of knowledge for practical ends, and even have different ways of classifying different types of knowledge than we in Britain. They do not have a set of, what turn out to be, distinctively English-speaking ideas about 'management' as consisting of a set of jobs set over and above other jobs. Nor do they have related ideas about professions or professional management. Indeed it is very difficult to translate these terms from English into the respective Continental languages.

The British evidence is considered first, mainly because it is likely to be of most direct interest to readers, and is dealt with in more detail for the same reason. Nonetheless, the position of the engineer in each of the countries is given a good deal of attention since it is apparent, on both numerical and practical grounds, that engineering forms the most important single occupation of executives in manufacturing in each of the countries.

The British executive

The evidence on the backgrounds of British executives, in the form of results of social surveys, is rather inadequate and patchy. No really comprehensive survey has ever been conducted, and although quite a lot is known about top executives in large firms, less is known about middle management, particularly in medium-sized and small firms. Also, much of the best evidence is dated and regionally based. The studies produced by the Acton Society Trust (1956), Clements (1958), and Clark (1966) are the principal ones considered here. Of these, only the Acton Society Trust study used a national sample. Further, relatively little has been done to explore general attitudes at the same time as routine data about education, family backgrounds, and careers have been collected. Significantly, almost all work on skills has been concerned with manual or clerical employees. Almost all evidence points in one direction. It fits, too, with the indirect data, such as that concerned with educational practices and trends, and initial occupational choices.

Education

It is doubtful whether there has been an educational elite among Britain's top executives. Insofar as one has existed, however, it has consisted of arts graduates from Oxford and Cambridge. Engineers and scientists have generally been recruited as middle-level specialists, rather than as potential top job holders. Also, educational achievement as such has not been as important for selection for top posts as it has been on the continent of Europe.

Virtually every survey shows that a public school education, or an Oxford or Cambridge arts degree, have been powerful assets for those who aspire to board positions. Yet these persons have not been the most able and ambitious products of the public schools and Oxford or Cambridge. Taken together, survey results indicate that it is their social backgrounds and skills, rather than their educational experience *per se,* that constitute their main assets. In the early-mid 1960s, only about one in three of all those in larger firms at the middle-management level, and above, was a graduate. Today, about 50 per cent of directors have degrees. In general, Britain's top executives in large firms are only a little more than half as likely to have higher-level educational qualifications compared with their Continental counterparts.

Even fewer have studied in subjects relevant to industry. Again, the content of courses in technical or other vocational subjects in Britain has generally been designed to produce middle-level specialists rather than potential top executives. Courses in engineering often appear to be aimed at producing academic researchers rather than enterprising executives.

Recent changes in higher education, in the establishment of so-called technological universities, and of polytechnics and business schools, have so far done little to alter the situation. Their courses in technical and scientific subjects are not on the whole markedly different from equivalent courses at the traditional universities.

More generally, academically able graduates from British institutions of higher education continue to eschew industrial careers, preferring to work in the professions, higher education, or the public service. Britain's universities, unlike some on the continent and in North America, have not provided industry with ambitious and able potential generalists with qualifications that are predominantly technical and commercial. However, educational attitudes on their own are not the key to this situation: the cultural and historical reasons for the low prestige of careers in industry in Britain have to be appreciated.

Professional and occupational backgrounds

Many British executives, apart from those with degrees, have qualified
by part-time study with the help of qualifying bodies. Accountants,
many engineers, and an increasing number of personnel specialists are
examples. Professional qualifying bodies are a particularly British
phenomenon. There are no equivalents on the Continent. They have
expanded in size and number from the nineteenth century onwards,
partly to meet industrial needs. They sought to remedy inactivity on the
part of the state and the universities, which had shown scant interest
in manufacturing. In some cases, for instance personnel management,
the training offered appears to have been designed mainly to compensate for what, on the Continent, would be regarded as deficiencies in
secondary education.

Partly because of the specialized nature of British professional
qualifications, those who have them have mainly regarded themselves
and have been employed as specialists in functional areas, rather than
as potential top job holders.

Professional institutions operate increasingly in the market for
graduates: but the response is partly a defensive one aimed to maintain
the attractiveness of the occupations concerned. Most British graduates
are not much better equipped with skills likely to be useful to industry
when they leave university than are school-leavers when they leave
school.

Those who have worked in finance, marketing, sales, and 'general
management' have reached top positions in British industry more
easily than those working in engineering, production, research and
development, and personnel departments. The former categories appear
to attract individuals with well-regarded social and educational backgrounds, who possess confidence and social skills felt to be necessary
for work at the board level.

Financial specialists are widely thought to be in short supply;
moreover, the accountant has the advantage of having a clearly defined
role and a specific area of expertise needed in order for industry to
function. Historically, cost-conscious administration has long been held
in high esteem in Britain, although the benefits appear at best to have
been uncertain.

The standing of personnel work has improved recently for a number
of reasons. Legislation affecting the industrial relations and training
fields has been one. Others have included developments in connection
with various effects of EEC entry, and a significant and interesting
tendency to follow US fashions. Thus the personnel director is

increasingly apparent and personnel specialists now comprise one of the best paid groups of executives. Unfortunately, neither financial nor personnel work can be regarded as central to the processes of making and selling three-dimensional artifacts. They may only seek to service and remedy defects in the process.

Engineering and scientific skills are, as noted, still widely defined in Britain as specialist ones. Those who have studied these subjects form the largest single group by education (but not a majority) in top positions. The engineer's situation is not the dominant one that it certainly is on the Continent. Production, manufacturing's main – and its distinguishing – function, is notoriously underpowered. It is poorly paid and young graduates avoid it for cleaner 'service' or 'staff' jobs in research and development, personnel, and so on. Experienced production executives who become business graduates appear to do so in order to leave this sphere of activity. Yet it is arguable that production should contain the most able group of those with technical qualifications, and the most able people generally, since it should be apparent that production is the most important single function in industry. The situation in Sweden has reflected this latter view for several decades.

Men with grammar school education behind them, and with high-level engineering and scientific qualifications, have moved into the ranks of middle management in large numbers during the last two or three decades. Yet, in most sectors, they have failed to get to the board room. Moreover, they appear to have been employed too often as technical specialists in research and development and management services departments, rather than in the more central production and design functions.

Critics have noted two reasons for this. One is the apparent unwillingness of graduates to work in production and design. Employers, perhaps unconsciously, use research and development and management services departments to attract graduates into industry before they are moved later into other functional areas (including production). The other reason is a tradition of 'arms-length control' by financial specialists, or by 'generalists' with little technical expertise, part of what has been described as 'an odd lack of concern with the product'. Those with technical expertise have tended to be shed in recessions, when there have been relative increases in recruitment of accountants.

A few other points about the occupational and professional aspects of careers are worth noting. First, mobility between jobs and regions has increased in recent years. There has been a growing trend for those trained as engineers, or as scientists, to move out of research and development work into other functional areas. Management services

and personnel work are two of the main examples; they have
begun to draw on a growing surplus of engineering and science
graduates. Finally, selection procedures have become more formal as
firms have become larger and personnel techniques more popular. As
will be implied later, however, they have not necessarily become more
rational.

Social backgrounds

In most countries it is very hard to separate the two influences of social
and educational background on the success of an individual, and
Britain is no exception. In Britain, however, social factors have
influenced education in a rather special way. Put very simply, education
has been valued more for its status value, rather than for its relevance
for competent work. And, as already suggested, evidence on the
educational and career choices of school leavers and graduates shows
that industry has not, on the whole, attracted many of the more
academically able products of the country's most favoured social
groups. Nor, for essentially social reasons, have the universities sought
to provide industry with potential executives who have been given a
mixture of a broad education and a training in sector-specific skills.

The response on the part of top job holders has tended to be
defensive and caste-like. For their middle level specialists, they have
relied heavily, until quite recently, on 'practical men' who came up the
hard way, either with or without part-time study. They promoted some
of these people into top positions, and in some other cases selected
'crown princes' with public school backgrounds or arts degrees from
universities, without job-relevant forms of training, but whose social
and educational backgrounds were felt to equip them to become (in the
Civil Service–Oxford jargon) 'generalists', or 'high-fliers'.

The Continental countries do not have 'generalists' of this type. In
describing the British situation, David Granick, probably the most
experienced commentator on European management, said in 1962 that
there are two sets of assumptions, amateur and specialist, in patterns of
recruitment to executive jobs in Britain. My generalists are his amateurs.
My specialists are those whose backgrounds, or experience, are felt to
be inadequate as a preparation for top positions. When such people do
rise to the top, it is felt that they have done so, on the whole, in spite of
their specialist backgrounds. They are the professionals or technical
specialists, who increasingly populate middle-level and some senior
positions.

The French executive

The evidence on the backgrounds of French executives is rather uneven in quality. Surveys are often restricted to particular industries or sectors, and they are often dated. Several are only concerned with top executives, and information on recruitment to middle-level positions is lacking. Additional data are often superficial and second-hand, and not much has been written about management styles or relevant aspects of the collective organisation of executives. There is, however, enough evidence overall for a general assessment to be drawn, especially as most commentators are in agreement.

France's top executive cadres probably contain the highest proportion of graduates in Europe: and careers in administration, either in industry or in the public service, are among the country's most highly regarded ones. The leading institutions in the old-established and very prominent non-university vocational sector of higher education, the *grandes écoles*, attract an intellectually more capable type of candidate than the traditional universities. These institutions train those who are widely regarded as being the elite of the country's future top executives and administrators. There are about 15–30 *grandes écoles,* according to interpretation, including those teaching business studies, veterinary surgery, arts and engineering. Among these, the engineering ones are very important indeed. Three business schools have *grande école* status. However, a large number of family-run enterprises do not employ many with educational diplomas, and the impact of higher education on the running of service enterprises has probably been slight. Nevertheless, a very high proportion of the larger and more important firms are run by products of the *grandes écoles,* and their influence is increasing across industrial sectors.

France is the country of the true 'technocrat', or high-level technical generalist, with men trained as engineers forming the most heavily represented group at the top in industry. They are notable for their famous career pattern of *pantouflage:* such men have often worked for a few years in the public service after completing their education, before they move into positions in the upper levels of industrial management. They are not the faceless, narrowly-trained type that the use of the term 'technocrat' tends to imply for Anglo-Saxon readers; and the successes of France's post-war 'indicative planning' appear to owe much to them. Following very rigorous selection and training, they belong, after qualifying, to a number of organisations enabling them to maintain close contacts with each other, and with their schools throughout their careers. Further, individual firms keep strong links with individual *grandes écoles,* as well as with the larger number of slightly less prestigious engineering schools, by recruiting heavily from them. It is not surprising, then, that they have been criticized for being elitist, and for forming an 'old-boy' network. In recent years a number of business schools have been formed, and some of these now appear to have *grande école* status.

To understand the situation properly, one should know something about the role of the French state, which set up a system of technical education, and industries, both before and during the time of Britain's first industrial revolution. The tradition of higher vocational education outside the universities is thus a very long one – and flexible, too, with new schools set up as new requirements became apparent. Course content is significantly more practical than is the case in Britain; education having taken much more responsibility for producing fully-trained graduates. The recent, successful establishment of business schools forms an important part of this tradition.

Higher education, especially in a *grande école,* is virtually a *sine qua non* for rising to the top of large firms, which clearly rely very heavily on educational diplomas when they recruit executives. In one survey almost 90 per cent of a sample of chief executives of the largest French enterprises had a university-level qualification, with 60 per cent of these being engineers by training, and 30 per cent having qualified in economics or law. Engineers, amongst senior executives, appear to be the best-educated group, having obtained university-level qualifications more often than commercial and other executives working at the same level. It has been suggested that executives with higher (but below *grande école*-level) technical training have 'posts' (*emploi*) and are selected accordingly to the technical needs of firms, whereas engineers from the *grandes écoles* have 'careers' and are selected 'by the logic of the political needs of the industry'.

There is evidence to suggest that in some industries engineers from the *grandes écoles* may not be quite as prominent as they were in the past. The products of the commercial *grandes écoles,* whose relative importance has grown since 1945, appear more often to prefer entrepreneurial kinds of career, such as those in export–import businesses, whereas diploma engineers from the *grandes écoles* most often begin their careers in the public service or in the public sector of industry. At least one survey shows that university science graduates fare far worse in industry than those who have attended an engineering or commercial *grande école,* or another engineering school; and they do not even do as well as those with a university training in law or an arts subject.

Another fairly recent trend is for big manufacturers to select their young executives more widely from the universities and business schools, as well as from the engineering schools, with the aim of getting a wider mix. As noted, an increasingly significant number are graduates of the commercial *grandes écoles*; as also are diploma engineers who have attended top business schools in France or America. Their members tend to work for international firms, rather than enter the French Civil Service. It is also worth noting that a fairly significant group of dedicated entrepreneurs lead their firms in less established industries: such men may be engineers or technicians by training, or they may be self-taught.

The social elitism of the *grandes écoles* system, its apparent rigidity, and disillusionment that it produces amongst university graduates, have all been subjects of considerable criticism. The social origins of France's top executives are severely limited: in spite of the overall growth in their numbers 'social inertia' at the top is very common. However, specialist functions are more open. In 1970 the government made it obligatory for firms to spend 1 per cent of their turnover on 'permanent education': this may be part of a series of changes that may, in the long run, make the reliance on diplomas less rigid. The *grandes écoles* 'system', of *'pantouflage'* and the 'old boy network' referred to above, operates most often and most efficiently in the Paris area. Recruitment in provincial firms appears to be more open, if less selective.

The system clearly has one beneficial effect, in spite of the criticisms. French manufacturing attracts a very good proportion of those who have been selected within the educational system as being the most able people of each generation; and the larger French firms are run, and led, by people whose education has been broadly relevant to their work. In both of these ways, France is very different from Britain.

The German executive

Research into the backgrounds of German executives, and into closely related topics, is, by and large, a fairly recent phenomenon. This is particularly the case for the evidence on social backgrounds, which further tends to focus on top executives. However, the evidence on educational backgrounds is fairly solid, although there is again a marked tendency to ignore middle and lower level people. The evidence on occupational backgrounds is more balanced than that on social backgrounds.

Some details of the German system of codetermination *(Mit-bestimmung)* can usefully be noted. It was begun a quarter of a century ago and consists of a two-tier system which ascribes certain functions to a body separate from the usual executive hierarchy. At the highest level of the latter, there is the executive committee *(Vorstand),* a collegial body with collective responsibility. It is responsible for managing the company's affairs, represents it to third parties, and is entrusted with the classical entrepreneurial function of risk-taking, subject to the supervision of the *Aufsichtsrat* (see below).

All public companies have supervisory boards *(Aufsichtsrate).* These consist of between 3 and 21 members according to the size of the firm's share capital. Two-thirds are elected by the annual assembly of share-holders; the remainder, who do not have to be union members, are elected by employees of the firm.

The functions of the *Aufsichtsrat* are, as the name implies, super-visory. Its formal powers are formidable but the usual custom is for it to go along with the decisions and policies of the *Vorstand.* Clashes over policy matters do sometimes occur between the two bodies, but the main functions of the *Aufsichtsrat,* in practice, are to appoint members of the *Vorstand* and to approve the latter's long-term investment decisions.

The composition of *Aufsichtsrat* stresses the interests of shareholders more than those of employees, although it does enable the latter to have more influence than they had hitherto. In some industrial sectors the *Vorstand* has to contain one labour director, who has the same status and responsibilities as other members while being mostly concerned with personnel issues. When insoluble differences over policy arise between the *Aufsichtsrat* and the *Vorstand,* the latter has to call a shareholders' meeting so that it can act as arbiter.

From the evidence on the backgrounds of executives, it can be seen that there are a number of educational routes to the top of German industry: law, engineering and business economics are the main ones. Over three-quarters of chief executives of large German companies are graduates of various kinds. Among the three main groups just men-tioned, the business economists appear to be gaining in importance whereas the position of lawyers, stronger in earlier stages of industrial development, is weakening.

As in France, engineers may be slightly less important than they once were, but they remain the biggest and most important single group. Germany is remarkable for the large number of graduate executives who hold a post-graduate degree: one survey reports that about half of the members of the executive boards of the very large firms have a doctor's degree. There is a very strong tradition of technical education for those at all levels of manufacturing industry.

Corporate management is not such an important feature of German business as it is, for example, in the USA. Owner–managers continue to play a role in German industry, in spite of a very high degree of concentration in certain major sectors. This is not only because some industries still mainly consist of small and medium-sized firms; it is also because some large companies are still owned by individuals or families. On the whole, however, German management is a mixture of old and new: no single factor is dominant. Instead, owner–managers appear to have been slowly losing out to employed people. Yet partly because of the persistence of owner–management, there remain strong elements of belief in the innate qualities of leadership, reflected in resistance to the use of 'objective' criteria for the evaluation of performance; and, more generally, resistance to Anglo-Saxon concepts of 'professional management'.

Executive work in manufacturing enjoys high prestige and attracts some of the best educated members of the higher social groups. Entrepreneurial families consolidated their position strongly in the years after the First World War and the destruction of the old order that had occurred. Nowadays the inheritors include salaried executives. A major effect of the Codetermination Laws of 1951 and after has been to make management styles more open, flexible, and less autocratic than they were hitherto.

As is the case with the French system, which they imitated in part, the German technical universities lie outside the traditional university system. They provide a technically-based general education and most of the original 12 technical universities are of international calibre. While selection procedures are not as stringent as in France, these institutions recruit a significant proportion of the country's most able school-leavers. More generally, German executives are almost as well educated as French ones.

The German system of technical education set the pattern for most of Europe. Until recently, the education system was a very rigid and traditional one, and social status and educational achievements matched each other closely. It provided a conventional, rigorous academic education for the more able at the secondary level, and education with a marked low-level vocational bias for others. A consequence of this was that for most of the present century Germany has had a large well-trained work-force at the skilled craft level.

It has been suggested that amongst the top executives of medium and large-sized German companies, rather over one-third are graduate engineers, and that of the remainder around 15 per cent are graduate economists and another 15 per cent lawyers. This overall assessment seems a fair one when compared with survey results, although the figure for lawyers may be a little high. Educational qualifications are very important for selection and promotion, but less so in small family firms than in others.

Although engineers are well represented in top jobs, however, large numbers of them are left behind in specialised technical jobs early in their careers. Again, as in France, natural scientists and arts graduates do less well in the promotion stakes in manufacturing. Generally, degrees are important and those who have doctorates fare better than those who only have first degrees. It has been said that a degree is a necessity for the employed executive, whereas for the owner–manager it is merely a correlate of his status. On the other hand, owner–managers tend to send their sons to the technical universities.

While business economists and lawyers fare better individually than engineers, this is mainly because the latter are much more numerous. As industrial work became more technical, and business economics graduates more plentiful, the importance of lawyers declined. But there are still lawyers, especially as chairmen, at the highest *(Vorstand)* level. Nevertheless graduate and other engineers dominate manufacturing industry.

An increase in the proportion of business economics graduates has taken place partly at the expense of non-graduates trained in the same subjects but at post-secondary vocational schools. Lawyers are to be found in greater numbers in large enterprises – the reverse of the situation for engineers. Although there is some mobility between firms, German executives rarely appear to change their occupations during their careers. In recent years recruitment has become more formalised, in contrast with the past when the entrepreneurial *(Unternehmer)* tradition was stronger. Appointment to the executive board *(Vorstand)* takes place when executives are relatively old by international experience: the average age is between 50 and 60. Indigenous German firms appear to have the largest percentages in Europe of men appointed to top positions late in their careers. Opportunities for younger men seem to be better in foreign-owned companies.

Men without university qualifications predominate in commercial jobs, but the position is changing as more graduates move into top positions. One writer has suggested that business economics training is inadequate and over-theoretical, but that engineering training is largely satisfactory. Generally, graduates have good prospects in personnel, commercial and technical work. Engineers dominate technical work almost exclusively. University-trained engineers are preferred for higher positions, and other engineers predominate in the lower ranks. Some of the latter have qualifications thought to be somewhat superior to British Higher National qualifications; others have qualifications roughly equivalent to the Ordinary National level.

Functional qualifications and expertise are important in the selection process at all levels, including the highest ones. Most executive boards contain between three and five members who are usually functional specialists; one of whom at least will be a commercial specialist, and at least one a technical specialist.

A number of conclusions can be drawn from evidence on social backgrounds. One is that German management is basically middle-class in character, although recruitment from the upper stratum of society is high enough to suggest that industrial careers carry a great deal of prestige. Members of the socially privileged classes are generally found in top positions, but the lower middle class is also a significant reservoir of executive talent. Recruitment into top positions from the lower class is nominal. The *Praktiker,* the man who rises from the shop floor, is losing out (as in Britain) to university-educated people. There is evidence of a fair amount of horizontal mobility between generations, between the civil service and industry especially; so in order to rise in manufacturing it is not fundamentally necessary to have an industrial family background.

The attitudes and styles of German managers are mentioned by a few writers. From this evidence, senior men appear to work long hours, partly because of an unwillingness, or failure, at the highest levels to delegate responsibility, and partly because middle-level jobs are probably understaffed. Hard work is a feature of the lives of most senior people in Germany. Traditional, more authoritarian standards appear to be clashing with more participative ones; and a self-conscious group of senior executives *(Leitende Angestellte)* who are felt to identify neither with capital, nor with labour, is emerging.

German executives feel that industrial careers are more prestigious than ones in the cultural and academic spheres. The authority of German management was formerly based on the idea of calling (complete identification with one's work), a belief in private property, and an elitist ideology: these values are now on the way out. There remains, however, a strong belief in a mixture of a broad, thorough training, combined with personal skill and flair, as keys to successful performance and promotion. Those who succeed do so as specialists who show ability to take on more responsibility; there is no sort of dividing line, as there is in Britain, above which individuals re-classify themselves as 'managers'.

The Swedish executive

Swedish data on backgrounds are quite up to date, and generally of good quality. Published evidence on the attitudes and styles of executives and on career mobility, however, is not so good.

Executive work in industry has enjoyed a high status in Sweden for most of the present century, although its standing may nowadays be a little lower than in previous years. Engineers are generally regarded as being amongst the most able products of Sweden's education system, as are the smaller but very significant group of business economists. Engineers are the most successful group for achieving top positions in the crucially important metal-working sector. Business economists are more prominent in light industry, and in large firms.

Modern industry came relatively late to Sweden, with most of the present largest enterprises having been formed in the first two decades of this century. The society is an old, relatively stable one, with a strong tradition of political and economic pragmatism. About half of the largest enterprises are in the metalworking sector, which exports about half of its output. Over 40 per cent of the country's total of manufactured exports consist of products of metalworking.

As in France and Germany, institutions of higher education that produce engineers, and some which produce business economists, are mainly separate from the universities: they are generally accepted to attract students of above average ability. So, although the education system has undergone a number of fairly important changes from the mid-1960s onwards, the separate institutes of technology enjoy a higher status than that accorded universities. Indeed, one British commentator, Hutchings, has argued that the two oldest-established institutes of technology, those in Stockholm and Gothenburg, are the Swedish equivalents of Oxford and Cambridge universities.

Before the first decades of the present century, many of those who reached the top in manufacturing concerns were lawyers: but as the importance of the metalworking sector grew, engineers became the dominant group. More recently, those with a qualification in business economics have begun to reach top positions.

The typical entrant into a large manufacturing concern continues to be a graduate in engineering who begins his career in production before making a shift to a job at the highest level, or just below it, in his thirties or forties. His studies have included a fairly heavy practical content and have been influenced by heads of department who have been recruited from industry rather than from the academic world. Middle and lower-level positions are populated by many who have received a technical or commercial training as a part of secondary education or at an intermediate level after a few years work in industry. As in France and Germany, the emphasis on broad vocational kinds of education is markedly stronger at all levels than is the case in Britain.

The managing directors of the largest firms are more likely to be engineers than members of any other occupational group, and such men are sometimes doctors of technology. Of executives in manufacturing at the level just below functional heads, over 50 per cent have a technical background, one-third have degrees in engineering, one-tenth have degrees in business economics and only 5 per cent have degrees in other subjects, including natural science. For every graduate in natural science, there are 30 engineers.

Some of the large manufacturing concerns recruit graduate engineers almost exclusively for future executive positions. These men usually begin their careers in production, which is regarded as the most important single function. Unlike many of their British counterparts, large and successful Swedish firms do not show much interest in doing basic research work; they are much more interested in technical development and in solving technical problems. And production, the main route to the top, is so strongly favoured that it is sometimes hard to get enough able people to go into product development. Marketing and selling are also regarded as very important. A hard-headed assessment of which functions are central, and which are not, underpins all this: so research and book-keeping are sensibly regarded as being of secondary importance.

Access to top positions is slightly more open in Sweden than in most other European countries, from the point of view of social origins, but less so than in the USA. There has been a tradition since the nineteenth century of selecting individuals for leadership on grounds of ability. However, a recent study showed that about 60 per cent of top executives came from 'upper' class backgrounds – which, however, probably overlap significantly with the British middle class.

By international comparison, Swedish management styles seem to be relatively pragmatic and democratic. Careers in manufacturing attract many of the most able products of each generation, and top executives in large and successful concerns are often well-known and accessible public figures.

Historical evidence suggests that management styles have evolved since the nineteenth century from paternalism to enlightened self-interest. Co-operation between industry and trade unions has been well-established since the 1930s, and there is currently a strong movement to involve employees in the organisation of their work. The strength and pragmatism of the trade union movement has been an important feature of Sweden's economic success and of the high degree of political stability. It is also notable that Sweden's professional-level and white-collar employees are the most highly organised in the world.

Discussion

More important than the fact that the Continental executive is more highly qualified than his counterpart in the United Kingdom is the fact that this education is far more relevant. Continental courses in engineering and business economics are designed to give a broad (as well as job-relevant) training to potential top executives. On the other hand, Britain's natural science and arts graduates, and even most of those with undergraduate degrees in engineering and management subjects, have been educated far more often with academic needs in mind.

In Britain, the more able student has traditionally been encouraged to eschew an industrial career. The reverse is the case on the Continent, so that British industry has never been able to rely to a great degree on the universities to help in the pre-selection of an elite of potential top executives.

Traditionally, too, the links between education and industry have always been closer in France, Germany and Sweden than in Britain. In most of Continental Europe there is a strong feeling for a cultural area of responses and habits associated with manufacturing that are quite separate from arts or science. This is *Technik,* a much broader concept than is implied in the English word technology, with its confusing and pejorative connotations of large scale and inputs from natural science. *Technik* translates broadly into 'the making and running of things', and it is distinguished in Continental minds from *Wissenschaft,* literally 'knowledgeship', which includes both English-speaking 'arts' and 'science'. To Continentals, *Technik* attracts entrepreneurs, participants in events; and *Wissenschaft* offers employment to clerks, those who observe and describe events.

Such differences between countries are hardly accidental: they are concerned with profound differences in attitudes towards the value of occupations and to the use of knowledge for practical ends. Consistent with these differences, there exists (for want of a better term) a 'Continental system' designed to staff industry with a good proportion of the most able members of each generation. In this system, potential top job holders have received a general yet rigorous secondary education, followed by a broadly job-relevant qualification obtained in the process of higher education.

This system can be regarded as the product of a sensible and straightforward approach to the need of a modern society to match education and jobs. The first response from, and even before, the time of the industrial revolution in each Continental country was to produce potential top executives trained in technical subjects at highly-prestigious technical universities, separate from the traditional university system. The second, the successful establishment of broadly-based business economics courses, was another rational response, this time to the growth in size of markets and firms since 1945. In each case the concern was with the product. As competition intensified and as markets became more distant and sophisticated, the need for good commercial and financial specialists was more important. It was still necessary to make a good product but it might no longer be enough to be overwhelmingly concerned with its production.

Production and sales/marketing are the two most important functional areas in manufacturing, and Continental practice reflects such a belief. A recent Swedish survey showed that 45 per cent of all job holders in production at the level below that of functional head were graduate professional engineers with qualifications close to the British M SC level, and that 85 per cent were qualified as engineers at the HNC-equivalent level or above. In Britain, however, production is both the least attractive function of all for the highly qualified, and one of the slowest routes to the top. A recent survey of Britain's business graduates showed that although 28 per cent had first degrees in engineering, only 3 per cent currently worked in production. Very few of our graduates enter production at the start of their careers. Only 6 per cent of the United Kingdom's chartered engineers work in production, whereas equivalent figures for France and Germany are probably four to five times higher.

Britain's system of matching education and jobs was not moulded in the philosophy that the needs of industry were very important; but was designed in Victorian times to provide jobs in the public service, or in the traditional professions for graduates of Oxford and Cambridge who had had public school education. It is not insignificant that W E Gladstone, that arch-proponent of moralism in public affairs, was the Member of Parliament for Oxford University for many years; and, as

Edward Heath, among many others, has remarked, many of those emerging from our universities today have been given an education more fitted to the administration of a vanished Empire than to running modern industries.

British assumptions about 'amateur-generalists', and 'specialists', were referred to earlier. Traditionally, middle-level specialists were those who came up the hard way, very often after part-time study. The educational correlates of the distinction are very important. The other three countries discussed have not, for example, encouraged an undue proportion of their best brains to be directed into scientific research, in the mistaken belief that natural science is the key to technical development in manufacturing. Continental engineering has not had to shelter under the wing of natural science in higher education. It has not had to fish in the wrong pool of talent because of factors associated with academic snobbery, and earlier specialisation at the secondary level. Moreover, Continentals do not misclassify, in a semi-literate fashion, engineers as scientists of a type. They are widely understood to be performing a more important function than the scientist, one that offers more personal fulfillment because it is closer to men's traditional and central preoccupations.

Both engineers and scientists are specialists in the British idiom, but more able school-leavers have been encouraged to prefer scientific to engineering disciplines when they apply to enter higher education. The reverse is the case on the Continent. British professional engineers are much more likely to have qualified via a part-time route than their scientific counterparts. Those who make things belong to the 'lesser breeds': wearers of white coats and writers of learned articles are felt to be more respectable. The skills of those who make heavy objects are not felt to be of the same order as those of the literate kind. Yet Continentals do not have 'specialists' in the British sense, defined as people whose backgrounds are thought to be unsuitable as preparation for jobs at the top. They have long expected their executives to qualify by virtue of their full-time education, and by developing personal skills in a specialism.

Their occupational associations do not need to give qualifications in order to fill a gap in education; there is no gap to fill. In consequence, partly-equivalent terms to 'profession' refer, on the Continent, to any occupation for which a person has to receive some form of training, be it that of lawyer, hairdresser, or airline pilot. In fact, the term does not translate easily into Continental languages. A French term, *métier,* which is partly equivalent, does not have the same connotations of social status, and sedentary work, that the British use of that word does.

Instead, it implies diligent use of specialist, personal skill and pride in the job, whether it be that of the baker pulling *baguettes* out of the oven, the engineer overseeing the factory, or the lawyer arguing his case with vehemence.

Anglo-Saxon ideas about 'professional management' were also referred to earlier. The 'management' idea has been used in the United States to help submerge ethnic differences, so that the accountant, the Pole, the production man, and the Greek could see themselves as *bona-fide* Americans. In this country, with its hopeful feeling for 'special relationships', and along with a host of fashionable 'management techniques', the idea has been mixed in with a set of confused ideas about 'professionalism', as a unifying concept for would-be members of an elite group. Just as the 'learned professions' always sat above the salt on the table, so too might engineers and other senior white collar people, through conspicuous consumption of formal qualifications and self-defeating chatter about their 'social responsibility'. None of these ideas have been popular in France, Germany or Sweden. Continentals have not had much use for management education. They have shown little interest in management science, which was invented in America and Britain before there was any body of systematic knowledge about the jobs of those whom it was supposed to help.

It is hardly surprising that, because of the haphazard nature of Britain's 'non-system', fashion and opportunism have been allowed to play too large a part in determining career patterns. This adds further to the low level of attraction of careers in manufacturing industry, in a situation in which those making and influencing choices have little direct knowledge of manufacturing.

Summary and prescription

Essentially the foregoing evidence and analysis shows that Britain lacks a modern system for ensuring that a good proportion of her most able people reach top positions in manufacturing industry. The original specification was wrong, and subsequent attempts to offer remedies have been half-hearted and more often than not misconceived.

At the beginning of the paper it was argued that management quality, rather than investment, was the key to understanding why British industrial performance has been inferior to that of the other three countries under scrutiny here. So if our industrial executives are less relevantly educated than their Continental counterparts, and perform

less well in consequence, why has this come about: and what can be
done about it?

First, there is the British belief in liberal market economics, which
does not readily allow for the State taking action to change an unsatisfactory situation. As we have seen, our labour market has not
worked to attract enough people of the right quality into manufacturing.
The French would never have expected the labour market to do the job
in the first place. The precepts of liberal economics have had a strong
influence on government policies.

Secondly, there is our habit of proposing shallowly-backed and
essentially gimmicky solutions to serious and complex problems. We
have lost the practice of going to the centre of things. Our 'generalists'
have been trained to hover around on the periphery, and our 'specialists' have rarely been granted sufficient mandate to get to the centre –
witness the naive expectation that scientific work will solve a manufacturing problem.

Finally, there is the belief in the United Kingdom that manufacturing
should somehow be rather low in the pecking order of interesting and
demanding jobs. Victorian complacency – a product of disorientation
caused by too much success – was an ancestor of this belief, as well as
of the other two causes mentioned.

The causes of the present situation are so deep-rooted that solutions
have to be basic. The following are suggested:

(a) the broadening of curricula in secondary education, with increased
emphasis on useful subjects and reduced emphasis on subjects taught
solely for academic reasons;

(b) the setting up of a small number of prestigious Continental-style
technical universities, offering broad and rigorous four year courses and
qualifications at MSC level. Their teachers should have substantial
experience in senior posts in manufacturing industry. New institutions
are recommended as the orientation of existing ones towards industry is
insubstantial;

(c) the setting up of a smaller number of similar institutions to those in
(b), to produce able and broadly educated commercial and financial
specialists through undergraduate education. If existing business
schools were adapted, they would need to accommodate major, almost
fundamental, changes in their aims and organization;

(d) comprehensive reform is needed in the education of engineers and
technicians below graduate level. As should be the case with all engineers, practical rather than academic requirements should predominate
in any action taken. One of the few positive features of British practice,
the possibility of moving up from one level of qualification to another

through further study, should be maintained where it exists, restored where necessary, and expanded where possible;

(e) the qualifying functions of professional bodies to be handed over to the universities, polytechnics and other institutions of higher and further education, working under the supervision of state agencies. So present British professional bodies would change their roles further in the direction in which change is currently indicated. Their work as monitors of training and disseminators of useful information could sensibly be expanded;

(f) the placing of a legal requirement upon employers in manufacturing to pay senior executives responsible for production and sales/marketing proportionately higher salaries than counterparts responsible for other functions. If this were not possible or acceptable, selective government support for firms should depend on the criterion being met.

(g) the distinction between 'administrators' or 'generalists' and 'professionals' or 'specialists' in the public sector to be effectively abolished for purposes of recruitment and promotion;

(h) the public sector should take a smaller proportion of the more able graduates than it does at present, and the practice of offering 'permanent' appointments or 'tenure' in the public sector and in higher education should be ended;

(i) all those employed to teach vocational subjects including academic ones in which research is undertaken, should be required to have been employed for a specified period(s) doing the kind of work for which they train others. This, along with the previous recommendation, would help to prevent the operation of a closed shop in most of higher education, and in the public service; and

(j) the above recommendations should be put into practice in ways compatible with other policies designed to facilitate two other related and desirable changes – namely moves in the direction of increased continuing education, and industrial democracy. Thus, access to senior positions should depend increasingly on job performance, and on the readiness of individuals to learn new skills during their careers. Similarly, those occupying senior positions should increasingly have to account for their actions and decisions to those affected by them.

To put these proposals into effect would not, it should be noted, necessarily be expensive. In the longer term, one aim should be to reduce the emphasis normally placed on age when individuals are recruited or promoted. More generally, flexible and skill- and work-centred attitudes towards careers should be encouraged by all those concerned with them.

References

British and comparative material: mainly demographic

Acton Society Trust, *Management Succession,* Acton Society Trust, 1956

Bambridge A, 'Why Britain can't manage', *The Observer (Business Observer),* 30 November 1975

Barnett, C, *The Human Factor in British Industrial Decline: an Historical Perspective,* Working Together Campaign, 1975

—*The Collapse of British Power,* Eyre Methuen, 1972

Beckett T, 'The hazards of professional indifference', *The Guardian,* 21 July 1976

British Institute of Management, *Front-line Management,* BIM, 1976

Business Graduates Association, *The Business Graduate in Britain,* 1973

Cairncross F, 'Breaking through the status barrier' (Interview with Sir Arnold Weinstock), *The Guardian,* 21 July 1976

Chisholm A W J, 'First Report on the Education and Training of Engineers on the Continent of Europe', Salford University, 1975

Clark D G, *The Industrial Manager: his Background and Career Pattern.* Business Publications, 1966

Clements R V, *Managers: A Study of their Careers in Industry,* Allen and Unwin, 1958

Fores M and Glover I, 'The real work of executives', *Management Today,* November 1976

Glover I A, 'Engineers – the forgotten profession?', *The Chemical Engineer,* January 1976

Granick D, *The European Executive,* Weidenfeld and Nicholson, 1962

Granick D, *Managerial Comparisons of Four Developed Countries: France, Britain, United States and Russia,* MIT Press, 1971

Hall D J, de Bettignies H-Cl and Amado-Fischgrund G, 'The European Business Elite', *European Business,* October 1969; 'Profile of the European Chief Executive and his American Counterpart', *Cross Channel,* July 1970

Hall D J and Amado-Fishchgrund G, 'The Chief Executive in Britain', *European Business,* January 1969

Heller R, 'The state of British boardrooms', *Management Today,* May 1973

Howie W, 'Remembering a golden age', *The Guardian,* 22 July 1976

Hutchings D, *Technology and the Sixth Form Boy,* Oxford University, Department of Education, 1963

—*The Science Undergraduate,* Oxford University, Department of Education, 1967

Reader W J, *Professional Men: The Rise of the Professional Classes in Nineteenth-Century England,* Weidenfeld and Nicholson, 1966

Scott W H, Banks J A, Halsey A H and Lupton T, *Technical Change and Industrial Relations,* Liverpool University Press, 1956

Stanworth P and Giddens A, (eds), *Elites and Power in British Society,* Cambridge University Press, 1974

Svensson N, 'It's respectable in Sweden', *The Guardian,* 16 July 1976

West Midlands Economic Planning Council, *Industrial Productivity – Scope for Improvement,* Midlands Tomorrow, Broadsheet No 8, 1975

French material

Delefortrie-Soubreyoux N, *Les Dirigéants, de l'Industrie Francaise,* A Colin, Paris, 1961

Fores M and Glover I A, 'Engineers in France', *The Chartered Mechanical Engineer,* Vol 23, April 1976

Hall D and De Bettignies H-Cl, 'The French business elite', *European Business,* Vol 23, October 1969

Monjardet D, 'Carriére des Dirigéants et Controle de l'Entreprise,' *Sociologie du Travail,* Vol 13, No 2, avril–juin 1972

German material

Hartmann H and Weinold H, *Universität und Unternehmer,* Bertelsmann, Gutersloh, 1976

Hutton S P, Lawrence P A and Smith J H, 'The Recruitment, Deployment and Status of the Mechanical Engineer in the German Federal Republic', University of Southampton, 1977

Kruk M, *Die Grossen Unternehmer,* Societatas, Frankfurt, 1972

Lawrence P, Glover I A and Fores M, 'Engineers in Germany', *The Chartered Mechanical Engineer,* Vol 24, October 1977

Pross H and Boetticher K W, *Manager des Kapitalismus,* Suhrkamp, Frankfurt, 1971

Zapf W, 'Die Deutschen Manager: Sozialprofil und Karrierweg' in *Beitrage zur Analyse der Deutschen Oberschicht,* Piper, Munich, 1965

Swedish material

Fores M and Clark D, 'Why Sweden manages better', *Management Today,* February 1975

Glover I A, 'Barely managing with academic qualifications', *The Guardian,* 4 February 1976

—and Fores M, 'Engineers in Sweden', *The Chartered Mechanical Engineer,* Vol 20, December 1973